# THE ANSWER IS STILL NO

## VOICES OF PIPELINE RESISTANCE

*EDITED BY*
**Paul Bowles & Henry Veltmeyer**

*VOICES OF*

| | |
|---|---|
| Shannon McPhail | John Ridsdale |
| Murray Minchin | Luanne Roth |
| Pat Moss | Karyn Sharp |
| Des Nobels | Nikki Skuce |
| John Olson | Jasmine Thomas |
| John Phair | Roy Henry Vickers |

Fernwood Publishing • Halifax & Winnipeg

Editing and text design: Brenda Conroy
Cover design: John van der Woude
Printed and bound in Canada by Hignell Book Printing

Published by Fernwood Publishing
32 Oceanvista Lane, Black Point, Nova Scotia, B0J 1B0
and 748 Broadway Avenue, Winnipeg, Manitoba, R3G 0X3
www.fernwoodpublishing.ca

Fernwood Publishing Company Limited gratefully acknowledges the financial support of the Government of Canada through the Canada Book Fund and the Canada Council for the Arts, the Nova Scotia Department of Communities, Culture and Heritage, the Manitoba Department of Culture, Heritage and Tourism under the Manitoba Publishers Marketing Assistance Program and the Province of Manitoba, through the Book Publishing Tax Credit, for our publishing program.

Library and Archives Canada Cataloguing in Publication

Bowles, Paul, 1956-, author
The answer is still no: voices of pipeline resistance / Paul Bowles & Henry Veltmeyer.

Includes bibliographical references.
ISBN 978-1-55266-662-3 (pbk.)

1. Petroleum pipelines—Environmental aspects—British Columbia. 2. Environmentalists—British Columbia—Interviews. 3. Enbridge Pipelines Inc. I. Veltmeyer, Henry, author II. Title.

TN879.5.B69 2014     665.5'44097118     C2014-900488-5

# Contents

Introduction

# Pipeline Journeys
## *Paul Bowles & Henry Veltmeyer*

At the time of writing, the National Energy Board's Joint Review Panel (JRP) has just published its recommendation that Enbridge's proposed Northern Gateway pipeline to transport Alberta's tar sands oil to the northwest coast of British Columbia should be approved subject to 209 conditions. The JRP public hearings were completed in June 2013 and the NEB decision — based on the National Energy Board Act and the Canadian Environmental Assessment Act — was released on December 19, 2013. The recommendation will go to the federal Cabinet for discussion. We do not know what the Harper government will decide, although given that the prime minister is on record that he will not accept "no" for an answer from the U.S. government to the proposed expansion of the Keystone XL pipeline, the signs are obvious and ominous and it would be a major surprise if the Conservatives turned their backs on their oil-patch supporters. The British Columbia government chose to defer to the JRP although did make a submission to the panel in which it declared that the proposal was unacceptable "as it stands". Since then, Premiers Clark of British Columbia and Redford of Alberta have been engaged in a merry public dance aimed at defending their interests but also in finding some common ground. A framework agreement between the two provinces was announced in early November. Nevertheless, there remains some uncertainty as the response to the JRP's recommendation by the B.C. government has continued to stress the importance of meeting its "five conditions," which are JRP approval, appropriate consultation with First Nations, world class land spill response capacity, world class ocean spill response capacity and a 'fair share" of the economic benefits for B.C.

But while the politicians' decisions are awaited, there is one certainty: the Enbridge pipeline will never be built. How can we be so sure? We are sure because the people of northern British Columbia and their supporters elsewhere will not let it happen. Some of the reasons why they will not let it happen are contained in the Voices in this book. From mail carriers and church singers to long-time activists, from self-proclaimed "cow girls" to First Nations leaders, the Voices in this book show the depth and breadth of opposition to the pipeline.

The economic, social, environmental and legal case for the pipeline is so weak and the strength and passion of the opposition so strong that the vested interests of "big oil" and their political backers will have met their match should they try to push the project through — just as other 'development' projects in the region — from Kemano II to fish farms to coal bed methane — have previously been halted in their tracks.

While the Voices and this book focus on the Enbridge pipeline, they speak to issues well beyond it. They speak to the limitations of the whole extractivist development model, now being pursued so vigorously by governments and corporations in Canada. The Voices question the legitimacy of this model and offer alternative ways of thinking about development based on local control and respect for the environment. This is relevant for many communities across Canada and elsewhere as well as for the next looming issue in northern B.C. itself — natural gas pipelines. The contributors share their views of how pipelines carrying tar sands bitumen and natural gas should be seen.

Included in the Voices are not simply the reasons for opposing the Enbridge pipeline, compelling as they are, but also the mechanisms for doing so. In our interviews we were keen to draw out lessons for other resistances. The interviews explore how civil society organizations work together, what mechanisms they use and levels they work at, what alliances they make and what niches they occupy. We explore how Fist Nations communities work together and with non-Aboriginal groups. None of this should be taken as problem-free. There are divisions within and between the various communities, Aboriginal and non-Aboriginal. Many of these have been caused by decades of colonialism with respect to First Nations communities and to differences of interests between labour and environmental groups for example. Of course, government and business do their best to exploit these differences, including Natural Resources Minister Joe Oliver's attempt to label opposition to the pipeline as the work of "foreign funded radicals". There are tensions in the pipeline resistance movement, as would be expected in any broad coalition, and some of these are evident in the Voices which follow. But far more noteworthy and inspiring are the solidarities, commitments to work together and overcome obstacles, shared objectives and passions, which come through loud and clear.

Before we hear the Voices, more on how this collection came about. When we started our journey this book was not part of the planned outcomes. We were undertaking research as part of a wider academic project on how northern British Columbia is globalizing. As part of this, we wanted to understand the opposition to pipeline development, especially the proposed Enbridge pipeline, just one of the many projects either actual or proposed in the region as part of the strategy to transport more of Canada's resources to the growing markets of Asia.

The Enbridge pipeline proposal is simply one high profile example of this

*Map 1: Pipeline route. Sources: BC government and Enbridge. Prepared by John van der Woude.*

broader globalizing thrust. The proposal is for two 1,177 kilometre pipelines to be constructed from close to Edmonton to the northwest port of Kitimat. One pipeline would carry 525,000 barrels of bitumen per day from Alberta's tar sands to the terminal in Kitimat. Here it would be loaded onto supertankers, 225 per year, for transportation to Asian markets for refinement. The other pipeline, flowing eastwards, would carry the condensate used to thin the bitumen for pipeline movement.

Although the pipeline proposal comes with the promise of jobs (how many is disputed), the overwhelming response to the project is negative, with 96 percent of the 9,500 public submissions to the JRP opposing the project. The JRP held public hearings in B.C. and Alberta for a year and a half starting in January 2012. The title of this book, "The Answer is Still No," comes from the rally held at the last JRP hearing, in Terrace in June 2013. A coalition of 160 First Nations have said 'no' to the project. Thirty-one municipal governments, two regional districts, the Union of B.C. Municipalities and six unions have passed resolutions against the project.[1] Public opinion polls have shown strong majority opposition.

Understanding the basis for, and dynamics of, this widespread resistance to the pipeline formed the basis of our research questions. We were interested in how the resistance had managed to draw so many supporters and what the basis of this support was, in terms of both the issues and its social basis. We were interested in how traditional divides had been overcome, how organizations worked together and how best to describe the resistance — as social movement? as civil society? We therefore decided to travel that part of the proposed pipeline route from Prince George west to Prince Rupert, some 720 kilometres away, shown in Map 1. We aimed to meet and interview people from organizations opposed to the pipeline.

---

1    See http://pacificwild.org/media/documents/press_release/our-final-argument-media-backgrounder-june-14-2013.pdf for a full list of the organizations.

Our starting point for identifying the people and organizations was the website http://pipeupagainstenbidge.ca.

We conducted interviews with nineteen people on our week-long journey. Twelve of them are Voices in this book. These twelve were selected on the basis of their willingness to be personally identified and their roles in the opposition to Enbridge.

We learned far more than we thought possible. Some of it we have published in other academic writings. But as we made our pipeline journey we also learned that many questioned the utility of academic work; others were more blunt and pointed to its futility. Publishing in academic outlets, laden with jargon and read by a few is all well and good, we were told, but how would that help the people we were interviewing and the cause for which they were fighting. Good questions indeed. This book is our attempt to provide an answer — to provide edited transcripts from the interviews, to provide a space for the Voices to speak to the broader world, to provide a record of their reasons for opposing the Enbridge project, to shed light on the mechanics of resistance and, perhaps most of all, to share with others the inspiration we felt in talking with these people. We hope that the power of their Voices comes through as clearly and strongly in the written word as it did in person.

The Voices we hear in this book appear in the order in which we heard them as we travelled from Prince George to Prince Rupert. The first Voice is that of Karyn Sharp, who works as a traditional knowledge research coordinator in Prince George. In her interview, Karyn highlights how the legal "duty to consult" with First Nations communities works in practice. This "duty" is required by the Crown but is typically delegated by governments to businesses, which must show they have "consulted" with First Nations communities over proposed projects on their lands. Karyn explains how this is a wholly inadequate process in many cases and deprives Aboriginal people of respectful input into decisions. It should, of course, always be remembered that in B.C. the vast majority of Aboriginal land claims remain unsettled by treaty, a fact which places First Nations in a unique legal position.

This point is also made by Jasmine Thomas, a young Dene women and member of frog clan living in Saik'uz. In addition, she highlights how an alliance of six First Nations, the Yinka Dene Alliance, has worked at local, national and international levels to bring pressure to bear on the Canadian government to take its responsibilities towards First Nations people and towards environmental sustainability seriously.

John Phair, from Burns Lake, provides us with some insights into the challenges of organizing in small communities. He speaks to the history of resource development projects in the area and the evictions which affected, and continue to affect, First Nations people today.

Travelling further west to Smithers, we first hear from John Ridsdale, Hereditary Chief Na'Moks of the Wet'suwet'en. He tells us of his responsibilities as a hereditary chief and the reasons why the Wet'suwet'en people have rejected all pipelines — oil and gas — on their traditional territory. He explains his responsibility to future generations and to the land, responsibilities which arise out of Indigenous law. In this respect, it is interesting to note that while Indigenous law places responsibilities on Aboriginal individuals and communities to protect Mother Earth, Canada and British Columbia do not specify any environmental rights in their laws. Indeed, while over a hundred other countries have specified constitutional environmental rights and responsibilities, Canada and British Columbia remain shameful laggards.

Next we hear from Nikki Skuce from ForestEthics, who outlines for us the four strategies the organization has been pursuing as a way of defeating the pipeline proposal. As a cross-border organization, she also outlines some of the issues that ForestEthics has faced, including being branded by the government as an "enemy of the state."

Pat Moss, an activist for the past thirty-five years, provides some historical context in her interview. She speaks of the many struggles in the region, including the successful campaigns against fish farming off the north coast, which would threaten wild salmon stocks, and the halting of the Kemano II project in 1995, proposed by Alcan to provide more hydroelectricity for its smelting operations but which would have threatened water levels in the Fraser River system and hence salmon stocks. Pat speaks to how First Nations and non-Aboriginal communities have a long history of working together on campaigns, of which Enbridge is just the latest.

In contrast to Pat Moss's long-standing activism, Shannon McPhail speaks of her conversion from a Harper supporter to a "common sense" opponent of the pipeline. This journey started for her when she learned more about Shell's proposal to drill for coal bed methane in the Sacred Headwaters. This is when her world was turned upside down and she came to see the damage that could be done by the type of development projects being proposed in the region, and she started organizing against them.

Roy Henry Vickers and John Olson come from the traditional territory of the Gitxsan, a community torn apart by a rogue chief's decision to sign an agreement with Enbridge, which sparked mass protests in the community, including the boarding up of his office. They share with us some us the challenges created by this situation. Roy's words offer a powerful case for an alternative way of thinking focused on the real value of nature and friendship rather than what he calls an addiction to the false god of money.

Murray Minchin, much like Shannon McPhail, came to take an organizing role in opposition to Enbridge from a non-activist background. When he heard about the pipeline proposal he started doing his own research and began to realize the folly of the plan, with oil transversing remote mountainous terrain via pipeline before being shipped through the hazardous Douglas Channel. He speaks to these follies and for the desire to keep B.C.'s northwest coast tanker-free.

This view is shared by the last voices on our journey, those of Des Nobels and Luanne Roth. They speak as two individuals with long histories in the commercial fishery, which has seen major changes as a result of the concentration in the industry as well as Department of Fisheries and Ocean (mis)management. They speak as Voices for a way of life under threat from many sources, including the pipeline and the tankers.

Taken together, the Voices presented here form a powerful testimony against the proposed Northern Gateway pipeline and in favour of forms of development which earn the "social licence" of the communities in which they occur by respecting the rights of First Nations, valuing the environment and benefitting local communities. While some projects have met this test and are peacefully proceeding, the Enbridge proposal resoundingly fails on these criteria, whatever federal and provincial governments may say, and will be resisted by communities throughout the region.

The resistance is about preserving some of the continent's last remaining pristine environment and the ways of life chosen by its inhabitants, and for many First Nations communities their territorial rights and survival as a people. The Voices speak loudly to these issues but they are a just a sample of the many voices in northern B.C. that we could have used, and they supplement the more public displays of resistance. They are part of a much larger provincial and national campaign. The rally in Terrace at the last JRP hearing has already been mentioned. Roger Annis, describes examples of other events:

> In Victoria, ... on October 22 [2012], 4,000 to 5,000 people rallied in front of the British Columbia Legislature to send a forceful message to the tar sands industry and its political representatives. "No tarsands pipelines across B.C.! No oil tankers in coastal waters!" read the lead banners. Two days later, thousands of activists staged rallies at the offices across the province of more than 60 elected members of the Legislature. Both actions were organized by the recently formed Defend Our Coast coalition.

The rally in Victoria was overwhelmingly Indigenous in appearance, participation and message.[2]

Like the rally in Terrace in June 2013, it was joined by community members and representatives of the local and a broader environmental movement. The rally, in effect, was part of a growing movement of civil disobedience as well as resistance. Annis continues:

> It featured a symbolic act of civil disobedience — the hammering of wooden stakes into the Legislature lawn, onto which a series of black cloths 235 meters long were attached, symbolizing the length of oil tankers ...
>
> In one of many stirring and militant speeches to the Victoria rally Art Sterritt, executive director of the Coastal First Nations, was reported to have asked, 'What are you willing to do to stop them? Are you willing to lay down in front of the bulldozers?' 'Yes', the crowd roared in reply. 'It's time to warrior-up', declared hereditary Chief Pete Erickson in another speech. He was referring to the warrior societies that have traditionally sprung up among First Nations people for self-defense. Grand Chief Stewart Phillip of the Union of B.C. Indian Chiefs told the crowd that Indigenous peoples stand shoulder to shoulder against the pipelines. 'We will fight this insanity through the joint review panel, in the courts of this country and, if necessary, at the barricades on the land itself', he said. 'We will not stand down, we will not step back. We will stop Enbridge and the Kinder Morgan proposals dead in their tracks'. ...

The rally message "No Pipelines, No Tankers"

> was carried into six public forums that took place across British Columbia in the following days. They were organized by the Council of Canadians. Four hundred people jammed into the Vancouver forum on October 25, which featured talks by Rueben George, grandson of Oscar-winning actor Chief Dan George, Bill McKibben, founder of the climate justice movement 350.org, and Caleb Behn, a lawyer, Indigenous resident of Northeast British Columbia and subject of the documentary film *Fractured Land*.

---

2    Roger Annis, "A Movement Against Tar Sands Oil, Pipelines and Tankers is on the Rise in Canada," The Bullet, E-Bulletin No. 720, November 2, 2012.

Maude Barlow, chair of the Council of Canadians and a leading spokesperson for a growing Canada-wide coalition of groups in the environmental movement, also spoke.

The Voices presented here are therefore part of a much wider movement concerned with the tar sands, with climate change and with extractivist development. While we are in no doubt that they will win their fight against Enbridge, it is but one battle in a larger war being waged around the world. Indeed, it is evident elsewhere in northern B.C. itself as the Tahltan First Nation's challenge to Fortune Minerals' proposed coal mine at Mount Klappan and the Tsilhqot'in First Nation's challenge to Taseko's "New Prosperity" mine project illustrate.

The Voices presented here from northern B.C. address one specific project but those voices are also are heard in many other parts of the world — coming from different mouths to be sure but the voices are still the same. In the Afterword we provide a brief overview of that wider global struggle.

# ~ Karyn Sharp ~

*Karyn Sharp is Denesuliné from Northern Saskatchewan. She works for the Carrier-Sekani Tribal Council (CSTC) in Prince George, B.C., as a traditional knowledge research coordinator for several proposed gas line projects in central B.C. She received her M.A. from the University of Utah in archaeology in 1999 and is a Ph.D. candidate at Simon Fraser University in archaeology. She taught at the University of Northern British Columbia for seven years in the First Nations Studies Department, focusing on traditional ecological knowledges, traditional use studies and land use planning. She also runs a small independent consulting company that focuses on training and capacity building in First Nations communities.*

*We met with Karyn in her office in downtown Prince George. The opinions expressed in the interview are hers alone and are not representative of any organization's official stance or perspective.*

---

*Karyn, could you tell us a little about Carrier Sekani's position, particularly on Enbridge and the decision to not participate in the Joint Review Process (JRP)?*

There's a different stance between oil versus natural gas. In terms of the oil, there is a clear, strong opposition because of what they see as an inevitable impact, not a potential impact. It will be a huge impact on the environment and the people; it is a matter of when the pipe breaks, not if.

I think it has been decided, given the whole environmental assessment, that the role First Nations are put in, as a common stakeholder, that they have chosen not to participate in that process because it doesn't fit with their accepted and supposedly government-backed recognition of Aboriginal rights and title.

*You are referring to being invited into the JRP as a stakeholder?*

Yes. Previous to that there was a different status for them (First Nations), they weren't just a stakeholder. They did have some slightly higher ranking than "the average citizen." And when that was gutted and taken away, that had a huge impact in terms of their willingness to participate.

*Has the decision of whether to participate in the Joint Review Panel or not been divisive in First Nations communities? Because many are participating even if it's to oppose.*

It's that whole question, do you participate and make your voice heard or do you just choose not to participate in the system? And some nations, given the shifts and changes, just chose not to participate. Within a lot of other First

Nations, I think most people would rather get their voice heard. And, a lot of people see it different ways. It's the ability to actually be able to have your voice heard. One thing they consider is that the EA [environmental assessment] process has taken on a role as verifying Aboriginal rights and title, saying, oh well, that's outside the scope of your rights and title, therefore your say isn't as significant. And that's not the role of the EA process. They aren't, at any point, supposed to be verifying rights and title. That is the given in terms of the Canadian Constitution. And so, many feel that this is not the area or role of the EA; the EA is purely about the environment and that's what it should be sticking to. Instead, it's choosing to take on a lot broader context in terms of Aboriginal consultation. That really is beyond their mandate.

*Part of the economic benefits Enbridge keeps promising is up to a 10% ownership stake. That must be tempting.*

Yes, there are a lot of First Nations that would really like to see that potential reached. They see it as a way to be able to have at least for an extended period of time, beyond the construction, having economic development occurring. And economic input occurring. I don't know anyone who has actually signed an agreement yet though.

*And how do they feel about the environmental damage?*

There's a lot of concern, an extreme amount of concern, given the salmon runs, the coastal water ways. We have all heard this in the news, but you know, we are talking about northern communities for whom a significant portion of the diet is still heavily dependent upon traditional foods.

*But would they accept putting it at risk for the sake of possible jobs or economic development?*

I know that there are a couple of smaller communities that don't have the numbers, don't have the land base, to really have a lot of other economic development opportunities. So, the opportunity to tap into something like that would allow them a greater economic development option than they would have just with Indian Affairs or any other economic development.

*And maybe they are not also as directly affected maybe because they don't have a big land base?*

Yes, they do tend to be a bit further south of the actual development. I don't know how much they've looked into in terms of watershed impact. But, in terms of the immediate impact of the corridor development, they do tend to be further south and further away from it.

*Do you think that solidarity exists with the communities that are more directly impacted negatively?*

That would be the ideal. Unfortunately modern politics have had a huge influence on Aboriginal solidarity, and everyone is scrambling for their piece of the pie. The whole treaty process, which puts down various strict boundaries and you have to negotiate according to those boundaries and government terms, and you only get a small percentage of that. People are expanding their boundaries, doing everything they can to try and increase that possibility that they will have in terms of negotiation. And of course, that puts them at conflict with neighbouring communities.

*So, the land claims process is a little divisive?*

Oh absolutely. You see all these decisions coming down from the broader federal government with really no consideration as to what's happening on the ground between these communities. And, it's very much entrenched in a western mindset. You know, clear boundaries, clear distinctions that don't often work well with Aboriginal communities, especially when you look at a lot of the smaller communities that have been formed due to the federal splintering. They were one nation and they [the government] said, no, now you are separate nations. You are dealing with forty or fifty years of trying to sort that out.

*Maybe the government prefers to deal with many different groups rather than a united front?*

Yes. There is certainly a strong perspective with most First Nations that it is a negotiating tactic by the federal government. You know, weaken your enemy, to their advantage.

*So, the CSTC decided to opt out of the review process and pursue legal avenues?*

I think so. But increasingly people have become aware of the slow route of the legal system. They know things get tied up for years, and meanwhile things are going through on the ground. The central First Nations here in B.C. have a long history of blockading and protesting against development within their territories, without their authorization. I would certainly see that as a possibility.

*You made a distinction earlier between oil and gas pipelines.*

Yes.

*With the oil one, is there opposition to just Enbridge, or is it Enbridge plus Kinder Morgan?*

It's plus. All oil. Enbridge is worrying because of its history and its consistent lack of safety that we see. But, it is oil as a whole, just because it is so damaging to the environment. When it gets in there, it's going to be damaging and have huge repercussions. When you are talking about the CSTC area, you are talking about the upper Fraser River. We really are at the point of the last bit of salmon coming in up the Fraser, and that's a very significant food resource for many of the core First Nations and for those around that Stuart Lake drainage area. And that would have a huge impact should anything happen to that. And, of course, the other major one is off the Skeena, coming off the coast. Those tend to be healthier fish, so to speak, as they are not as worn out as coming all the way up the river. So, they are extremely valuable, and there is an extensive trade network among First Nations, even today, to get those Skeena salmon further interior. Anything that would potentially damage them would be a huge loss to the communities.

*Probably, the company will say that the technology now is not going to let it happen; that there's very minimal risks. But pipeline history suggests otherwise.*

Yes, and First Nations are certainly aware of the spills, especially in the U.S. So, I would imagine that they would certainly take a broader global scope as well. And, like you said, I don't think there is any example of a pipeline that hasn't had safety issues. It is a matter of when it breaks, not if it does.

*Does the Council draw on academic expertise?*

Oh absolutely. Yes. Within the council themselves, within their lawyers, and then working collaboratively with a couple of institutions. There are many trained individuals within the populations they can rely on.

*What about activities outside of the region? I am thinking about some of the work that Chief Terry Teegee has been doing going to Europe and to U.N. meetings?*

The CSTC are certainly broadening their scope as much as they possibly can and have been working with the U.N. and using the U.N. Declaration of the Rights of Indigenous Peoples Policy.

*The idea that taking it to a global scale, who is that to pressure? Is that to pressure the Canadian federal government?*

It's definitely to pressure the federal government. There is a certain sense of solidarity with other Aboriginal peoples around the world. But, it's widely recognized that Canada doesn't have a very good record in terms of its Aboriginal consultation and Aboriginal policy. And so, bringing it to the larger global scale it increases the pressure that is put on Canada. And we have seen that already occurring with some of the U.N. visits that have happened and are scheduled to happen. That is certainly a strategy that the CSTC sees as an effective one.

*What's the difference between oil and gas pipelines?*

The gas has less of, or is viewed as having less of, a long-term environmental impact. It's pushed through, at least the proposals that I have seen, is being put through as a gas, in gaseous form. So, if there is a leak, it will basically evaporate in a fairly rapid period of time. And so, it doesn't have the long lingering effects that it would have if it were oil or bitumen. And so, there is less opposition to it at least in terms of the potential environmental damage. The approval for these projects hasn't been given by many First Nations yet as it is just now being explored, but the immediate concern is not like what we are seeing with oil/bitumen. The concerns are ultimately still making sure that it's done in a respectful way. Making sure that it's done with the least amount of impact on the environment, trying to ensure meaningful consultation between all parties. Those are three of the things that First Nations really ultimately want, irrespective of what the project is. They want to have that occurring with industry. The gas is viewed as less harmful ultimately in the long-run. It's not that First Nations are against economic development or industry development. It's having it done in a respectful and appropriate way. And, if that can be achieved then Aboriginal people see the benefit of it. They see the economic benefit for the nation and for themselves and for the broader Canadian government. And they are willing for that to occur. But, it just needs to be done in a way that is listening to the First Nations peoples.

*So it's purely an issue of what goes in that pipeline then? It's not the issue of say, tar sands and climate change and fracking?*

They are not happy with that at any point. They certainly are largely against the tar sands and the fracking they are not for because that causes a lot of environmental damage and they have seen that. Fracking, at least in terms of the CSTC area, isn't proposed at this point. In terms of the pipeline itself, yes, it's what is going through it, what is being transported through it.

*Land use planners at the CSTC, do they also bring into their purview the water resources or look just strictly the land?*

It's the water as well. They have a big initiative right now to try and rehabilitate the white sturgeon. And so, water is certainly a big component of that. And there is a lot of concern about the water because of the damming system.

*Does this spill over into site C?*

There are a lot of concerns about the site C because it does impact the communities, and of course, the watershed system affects many of the communities within the CSTC boundaries.

*How would you describe the opposition to the Enbridge pipeline? Is it little pockets of opposition, loosely linked together, or is there some broader coalition?*

I think there is a broader coalition. I think there's a fairly large alliance of First Nations who are in opposition to this, and there tend to be little pockets of people who don't necessarily agree with that stance.

*Would you say that the Enbridge pipeline issue has in some sense enabled Aboriginal and non-Aboriginal groups to work closer together than they have in the past?*

I think Enbridge has certainly been a rallying point, yes. I think it has, at least, brought the varying groups together on an agreed-upon stance, which has been attempted in the past, such as in forestry. But, forestry usually ends up being divisive within itself. So, I think the oil proposal has managed to unite the different groups together.

*All these groups, the non-Aboriginal groups, is their sole concern generally with the environment or do they, like the Aboriginal populations, also have concerns over livelihoods?*

I think it's a mix. I think in terms of the majority of it is the environmental aspect. I have seen several discussions by municipalities and other organizations about not seeing the long-term economic benefits, and so there is a concern about what its impact will be on the communities, the non-Aboriginal communities as well. But, I think the majority of it is definitely environmental.

*While non-Aboriginal communities may concentrate on environmental and economic impacts, for First Nations it's much more complicated in that it's got process issues around respect for Aboriginal title, as well as the cultural dimensions of the salmon?*

Yes. It is impacting many different aspects of our lives. It's the whole thing from the initiation of the project all the way through the approval process, all the way to construction and then ultimately to the decommissioning. The fact that all of these projects are all developed without any insight of Aboriginal communities from the get go. The model is, "we need to get from A to B, we are going to do it the most economical way and then afterwards, what First Nations were consulted, what might the impacts be?" Instead they should start by saying, we want to get the gas or the oil from here to here, and then start working with the First Nations from the beginning. None of that ever happens. We are always brought in after the initiation process of the project itself.

*You are always placed in the position of being an obstacle to something?*

Yes. Exactly. And, the consultation only happens because it's mandated. If it weren't required by the federal government, in all honesty it wouldn't happen. I'm working on this project right now, and the timelines on it are ridiculous. The amount of expectation for not just one community, but in this case, two to three different communities to come together and make a decision on a pipeline that is going to be coming through. You have to assess the project, talk to the community members, make a decision, write the reports and do it within basically a three-month period. And, you are not talking about communities that have the capacity to do that. And, yet, the companies are like, "no, we want to be the first one to get the EA process started." And so, they just push these timelines and it's causing huge distress in the communities. You don't want to miss anything. You are being rammed on one side, saying you have to do it, you have to do it. There is a vagueness in a lot of these projects as well, "we think this is the route it is going to go and we think it's going to have a right-of-way this long, but we don't know exactly."

*Can the company actually impose these deadlines?*

It seems to be that they can. Yes, ultimately a lot of the funding that is coming forward for the studies comes from the pipeline companies themselves. And so they want it done by a certain date, and beyond that they won't provide any additional funding. And, the First Nations, I mean the CSTC because they work collaboratively, have a bit of a bigger economic pool to pull from, but there's a lot of First Nations that aren't part of the CSTC and they don't have that economic pull to be able to hire consultants and do what they need to do.

*So a company will come to you and say, we are proposing a pipeline, whether it be oil, gas or whatever, going through some of your territories. We are consulting with you, please tell us what impacts we have to mitigate or whether you agree and we will give you so many thousand dollars to do studies to support your case, and we need to know by date x.*

Yes.

*That's the reality of what constitutes consultation?*

Yes, it is. It's not at all what one would define as meaningful consultation. You've got the process exactly right. That's what ends up happening, and a lot of times the companies say "Review these maps, look at our reports and see what you think." And sometimes they don't even provide funds for traditional use study; it's just "This is what we've done, what do you think? Do you think this should be approved? Or are there concerns that you have?" And, "Oh yes, we need the response within the next four weeks."

*What happens at that point if you just say, "Sorry, that's not enough time. We don't approve."*

It goes through anyway because the company views it at that point as they have attempted to consult.

*So you don't need agreement, you need consultation?*

Correct. The company made the effort and if the First Nations chose not to respond then they say well that was their decision. And the government takes it as, well, you made the attempt to consult.

*Do you think that the pipeline will happen?*

The Enbridge pipeline? Personal opinion, I go back and forth. Part of me is inclined to say no. I view it much like the Mackenzie Valley Pipeline that was an initiated and planned in the late sixties and the seventies. You are still dealing with a lot of the same issues that they dealt with in the Mackenzie. The Mackenzie eventually got approved but it still hasn't been completed or constructed all the way through. And there is still a lot of opposition. So, I see the Enbridge Pipeline following a very similar route because of its lack of adequate consultation, the strong concerns, the environmental concerns by many of the First Nations. I see it as being caught up in a lot of long-term court disputes. Now, having said that, we also know Harper isn't the most responsive to political or social concerns. So, I could see him allowing it to go through. I think there will be a lot of opposition. I think it will get tied up in the courts and you will probably end up with sections of it built and it just never being completed, at least for another twenty years or something like that. I mean, Mackenzie Valley, it's thirty years on and it is still caught up.

*There has been quite a long history of pipelines — Mackenzie Valley — and also a long history of mega projects in B.C. from the Bennett Dam and Alcan, for example. Do you feel that you have more tools now to fight these projects?*

I think we do, yes. There's a much stronger sense of the legal system. A lot more capacity within the Nations to fight the system. We have built on the experience that we had in the past. Of course, when a lot of those big mega projects came through, the ones that you mentioned, it was a different time economically for our Aboriginal communities. There was still a lot of people who were doing, for lack of a better word, seasonal rounds, and who weren't necessarily in one location. When you look at the world today, a lot of Aboriginal people, we are much more sedentary than we ever were thirty, forty or fifty years ago. And so, I think in terms of the awareness of the communities, it's a lot more significant now than it was fifty years ago.

*That's interesting because you often hear the opposite, of the trend to urbanization and of the urban Aboriginal population now being greater than it is on reserves.*

Certainly, but the fact that people are on the reserve now, they are not necessarily out in the bush trapping, they are not doing the seasonal activities off the reserve. Whereas, fifty years ago they were. They would have been out in the bush hunting and trapping, and the reserve was a place that you came to periodically or stayed for several months at a time. But now on the reserve, people are there. And so they are much more aware of what's going on. They are seeing what is going on and sharing that information among each other and their neighbours. People are sharing the information a lot more freely than they did in the past. And many of the people in urban areas are trying to preserve their traditional lands as they want to be able to come home, to a clean home. And, of course, they are much more globally aware. It's not to say they weren't globally aware fifty years ago, but the awareness has certainly increased exponentially.

*What about the various training programs for pipeline workers? You've been involved in some of those, I think, haven't you?*

Well, there's always the push to do it, yes. How they actually follow through in the end has been very questionable. A lot of times the training tends to be just the minimal basic lower level skill building, the quickly learned skills, and it tends not to branch out into higher skill sets for many of the First Nations. And so, there is a lot of hope there. You have agreements with pretty much any industry that you can imagine within this territory, allowing for economic training and skills training for the community members, but what actually ends up happening tends to fall very short of the agreements.

*The training is offered through both government sources and industries funding isn't it?*

Yes.

*Does that place you in a difficult position about whether to accept that given that some of the training to build a pipeline, and who knows what's going through it? Is that a problem for you?*

Not that I've ever heard, because we recognize the skillsets are broader and, for example, welding, you might be welding for a pipeline, but welding has broader applications. And again, it's ultimately what is going through the pipeline versus economic development per se. First Nations are not opposed to economic development. It just needs to be done in the appropriate manner. And if they can get training and the skillsets and build the capacity, people will do that.

*Are there big differences between gas pipelines and oil pipelines? Is there a possibility of using the same pipeline?*

No, you can't use, from my understanding, you can't use the same pipeline. Well, at least with the Enbridge proposal, it's two pipelines, one pushes out, one pulls in. At this point the proponents for the liquid natural gas (LNG) pipelines are saying that they cannot be modified to allow for oil/bitumen later. Whether this is true or not I am not sure. From my understanding, right now we have, not even counting Enbridge, six proposed pipelines through this area and these are all LNG. And each one is proposing a separate gas line. So, you don't even have collaboration within the different liquid gas lines using the same pipeline. Instead you are seeing six separate pipelines being constructed, and that's a concern because you've got huge cumulative impacts. Okay, we have got one pipeline here that has, say a fifty metre stretch right-of-way on either side, now you've got another one that is running parallel. So, all of a sudden, now you've doubled to two and you've got three or four more and you are already looking at exponentially increasing your right-of-ways and you are talking about a swath of right-of-ways and pipelines that is two kilometres wide, right through First Nations territories. That's a huge impact.

*Would you have to have six? Couldn't the Council look at it and say, which one of those could be approved and which ones could not?*

Well, certainly, they aren't likely to approve all of them, and realistically I don't know if all six of them will go through. But you have to look at them all, this is what they are faced with, there are six proposals being put forward. You can't just presume that necessarily all of them, or only one of them, will go through. Personally, I don't see why the companies don't collaborate and come up with a division and have one pipeline and split the gas that gets piped through.

*Presumably the companies are in the position of whoever gets approval first captures the market.*

Yes.

*As they all know there is not enough demand in Asia for six pipelines, but it's the first mover advantage.*

Exactly. And that's what we are facing with the timelines, we need this information now, three months from now, because they want to be the first ones to get their application in to the EA.

It's just hard to imagine. If six of them went through, how on Earth would that happen? Even if you took half of that, three of them, all of a sudden, now you have economic development in the north, which has largely been unimpacted by a lot of these economic developments. You are going to have to have a significant amount of infrastructure development, which in itself isn't necessarily bad, but you are talking about roadways. You are talking about energy, water being piped into these areas, and of course, once you build these roadways it expands access for other possible industries to expand into these areas as the infrastructure has been established. That has a huge impact in terms of increased hunting and pressures on the animal population and the fish population and water.

*In terms of the politics of the pipeline proposals, I don't suppose there is any possibility here, like there would be in some Latin America countries, of the companies making all kinds of offers, to get approval?*

Oh yes. There will definitely be that. That happens with pretty much every project. Someone goes up to a First Nation within a community and tells them, where can I find the chief and what do you think about the pipeline? Oh great, here's $1500. That's considered consultation by many of the companies. This is happening with people and communities I've worked with. So, you know, people will take the broadest scope in terms of what consultation means, and certainly economic initiatives or incentives are definitely a part of that.

*Is there any possibility, again like in Latin America, of the formation of an Indigenous movement to mobilize the resistance?*

No, not nationally. There have been pushes locally to try and get one going, the Yinka Dene Alliance has been a big push on that. I haven't seen anything like that occurring in Canada outside of the sixties and the early seventies. There really hasn't been a national move towards unification. There were attempts last year with the Idle No More resistance but that even has died down this year.

The only thing that seems to be potentially consistent across the many different nations at this point of economic development is fracking. Because that is occurring from east coast to west coast and north to south. It's occurring up in the northeastern part of B.C. It hasn't reached into our territory yet. I wouldn't be surprised if it would eventually be proposed for our territory. But, I will also say fracking is such a new process that it really hasn't had the time to gather that momentum yet. But, you hear about a lot of moves out in the east because of the big push up in the shield area. And of course, here in B.C. it's starting to really push forward, and we are seeing it in Alberta as well. So, I think if it continues, if this is a process where the government or industry doesn't back off, that might potentially be unifying because it will affect all First Nations across Canada.

# ~ Jasmine Thomas ~

*Jasmine Thomas is a young Dene woman and Frog Clan member living in Saik'uz which is her mother's traditional territory, located in the heart of what is known as British Columbia. She has been actively engaged in resisting the proposed Enbridge Northern Gateway tar sands pipeline project, which would impact her own and surrounding communities. Jasmine has worked with groups such as the Yinka Dene Alliance, Indigenous Environmental Network and Indigenous Tar Sands Campaign. In her community she works on numerous environmental health, cultural and land-based projects with youth and other knowledge holders.*

*We met with Jasmine in Tim Horton's in Vanderhoof. The views expressed in this chapter are her views only and not necessarily those of any organization.*

---

*The Yinka Dene Alliance has been involved in organizing opposition to pipelines. Could you start by telling us about how the Yinka Dene Alliance came about, how you became involved, and who else is involved?*

Sure. My name is Jasmine Thomas. I am from the Saik'uz First Nation. First, some background on how the Yinka Dene Alliance came to be: Enbridge came into our communities here around 2005 with their proposal. Different communities got support from Carrier Sekani Tribal Council to start doing our own baseline studies and look at the proposed impacts, not just environmentally but socially as well; how it could impact our culture and our way of life. After doing the research, the Aboriginal Interests and Use Study was prepared, and the communities decided from there that the risks that were involved with the project were too great for our communities. We are still experiencing forms of colonization, the legacy that is still living in our communities, experiencing the loss of our language, and other important parts of our culture. Even though the communities were unanimous in saying no to this project from the beginning, Enbridge went away for a little bit, but then they came back thinking that they could get this project forward, that they could receive support from some communities. The Yinka Dene Alliance started off with three Carrier communities here, the Nadleh Whut'en, near Fraser Lake area, Nak'azdli, located around Fort St. James, and Takla Lake First Nation, located in the northeast. They were the first original members, and then other communities, Saik'uz and Wet'suwet'en First Nation, then lastly Tl'azt'en Nation joined and formed the Yinka Dene Alliance, and I think we needed to come together and unify our voices to let Enbridge know that we have done our homework and that we are still opposed to this development. We are going to use whatever means necessary to make sure that this project doesn't threaten our future.

*Every means?*

Every means possible, using whatever tools we have available, domestically or internationally.

*So, Enbridge came into your communities. Did they speak to the chiefs? How did they go about their strategy?*

Their strategy was having an Aboriginal liaison to try to engage with the communities along the way, sending a person literally throughout the communities.

*It has to be an Aboriginal person that they would recruit for this purpose?*

Yes, to get support that way.

*How would this liaison person contact the community?*

Literally by going to the band offices or trying to make direct contact with chiefs. But, I think our communities were keeping a close eye on them as well, and it's like, okay, we have spotted them, they are just leaving this community. And then keeping an eye on where they are going.

*Originally, some of the communities, I'm not saying any of yours in the alliance, but some First Nations communities, actually signed on initially, didn't they?*

Yes, and I think that is a lot of Enbridge's way of trying to say that they have support, but it's not understood in that way, I think, by the communities. Some communities signed protocol agreements of how they would communicate with each other and so that communities can do their own studies, and then Enbridge turns it around and says we have the support of so many communities. But, it's not the truth that they are putting out to the public and to media.

So, like I mentioned, we will oppose the project using any means necessary, not just through Canadian law but through our Indigenous laws as well. Once the Yinka Dene Alliance was formed around 2010, we felt that this is not just an issue for our communities here in the north. Twenty-five per cent of the pipeline route would come through our territory, of the collective YDA communities. We thought it was a good strategy to start making connections with other communities who are also depending on the waters that connect us all. So, the Save the Fraser Declaration came about. It is based on Indigenous laws and led to banning not only this particular oil pipeline project, but also other tar sands development projects that could not only impact our communities, but also others along the entire Fraser River watershed. We have been experiencing great declines in our salmon stocks, and a lot of our communities do depend on food that comes from the water. So, the Save the Fraser Declaration started, I think it was about 30 or so communities that jumped onboard along the Fraser River, and then it started to grow each year. As of 2013 we have over 160 First Nations that have signed on to the Declaration.

All along the pipeline route as far as the Northwest Territories to the Arctic Ocean, including nations from other North American Indian tribes as well. Basically what it looks like is the whole entire coast of B.C. along the Rocky Mountain border, the Northwest Territories on top, and then the U.S. border. So, it's like Enbridge is totally surrounded.

*You have taken the view that it's not only the proposed Enbridge route, as it is, but with any deviations from it that Enbridge might propose up through the north?*

Exactly. We are also making those connections with communities who are being directly impacted by tar sands, downstream, upstream, as far as the Northwest Territories communities, and then other nations, American Indian tribes in the south, who are opposing the controversial Keystone XL pipeline. Indigenous peoples across North America have started to come together with a unified voice, not just on the Enbridge Pipeline project, but the Keystone XL and Kinder Morgan projects, which are all connected through the veins of this tar sands master project, and we work together in different ways.

Different approaches have been taken. I know the Yinka Dene Alliance, even before the alliance was formed, our communities have been asking for a separate First Nations Review process. Currently, the federal government process doesn't recognize the cumulative impacts associated with this project and that was one of our major concerns. The impacts of climate change and the expansion of the tar sands are not considered. How is this project affecting Canada, and what impact is Canada having on the world by increasing this very unsustainable development? The federal government hasn't made any attempt really to respect a separate First Nations Review process that respects Aboriginal rights and title, those cumulative impacts and other things like that. But, internationally, there's different legal instruments, like the United Nations Declaration on the Rights of Indigenous Peoples, ensuring that free prior and informed consent is there for our communities, but there is no free prior and informed consent. They are not respecting our ways of how we govern ourselves here and because of the lack of treaties in the area, we are still the sovereign stewards of this land. There is no bill of sale to say that they are allowed to proceed.

So, we can use domestic and international legal instruments but also taking other various forms of action such as non-violent direct action. A lot of our communities have become frustrated trying to use every means within the Western system. Now we have to get creative to try to get the message across. There was a lot of networking with people directly on the ground, who have been already impacted by other Enbridge projects as well. We have been on the front pages of the media for various protests and rallies. There are other ways as well such as the Idle No More movement, which has sprung up recently and is finding peaceful ways to show that we are still here living, our cultures are still here and alive. We are using various tools, like social networks, like Facebook, Twitter, to get our message out because a lot of our opposition was not being shown in the media initially.

Our communities have boycotted the Joint Review Panel hearings because of the reasons I outlined. It's very evident that it's not just the First Nations communities, the Yinka Dene Alliance, but Canadians in general who are opposed and who have stated that. Our chiefs have mentioned that they would put their bodies on the line. They will be in front of those bulldozers, but we don't want it to get to that point. Some other approaches that we have taken are in the international community, going to the United Nations, to the climate negotiations there; making sure that the international community puts pressure on a country like Canada, which claims to have the highest environmental standards and the highest human rights standards. It was a struggle just to get Canada to adopt or even recognize the United Nations Declaration on the Rights of Indigenous Peoples. So, we started from that and put pressure on Canada for its role in the climate crisis that the world is experiencing now. We attended the United Nations for those reasons. We have also recently met with the U.N. Special Rapporteur on the Rights of Indigenous Peoples, James Anaya, over our second submission to the United Nations for Canada and British Columbia's violations of International Law. We've been to the European Union. I have personally testified in Parliament there ...

*In the European Parliament?*

Yes, in Brussels, Belgium, with other doctors who have done amazing work with communities in Fort Chipewyan in getting the information out on the increases of cancers and other things happening in those territories. We have been working with medical professionals, legal professionals, and going to these places. We did see some success with the Fuel Quality Directive that the European Union has been working towards. That has meant a lot in our struggle, having the international community recognize that tar sands bitumen is not the same as conventional oil; there is a big difference. How this project is being looked at and being assessed in Canada is not considering the difference between bitumen and conventional oil, but the world is starting to recognize that there is a difference. Along with those paths, we have targeted different stakeholders, such as investors, by attending the shareholder meetings that Enbridge holds annually. We are talking to the shareholders about the risks that are associated with the project telling them that we are very concerned and that investing in such a project is futile because our communities will never allow it to pass. We reach out to the shareholders of the company itself, but also to the financial community. We did a campaign, nationally, where we went to every major Canadian bank and went to their shareholder meetings.

*Was that just the Yinka Dene Alliance doing this campaign?*

We weren't the only ones doing this campaign. There was the Yinka Dene Alliance, but we worked with organizations like the Indigenous Environmental Network and went internationally as well and reached out to the Royal Bank of Scotland and their shareholders, but with other communities like Fort Chipewyan, Little Buffalo and Beaver Lake Cree, who are living directly in the tar sands areas. So, it's not just the Yinka Dene Alliance but other impacted communities around North America and South America as well. We have been meeting with delegations from Ecuador and going to the Gulf Coast of Mexico. My mother, Geraldine, went there and saw the devastation where attempts to clean up oil would be useless, and met with different tribes along the Gulf Coast area, including the Houma Nation, but also with people from Ecuador who wanted to share their experiences with the fossil fuel industry as well. We have very diverse pathways to address this issue.

*When you say pathways, pathways to address the issue of corporate power?*

Yes. That would be it. It's just one project that we are talking about, but there's so many different projects bombarding our communities, be it in forestry, in mining, in different energy kinds of projects. When dealing with this company, Enbridge, there's a lot on our plate already, especially when many of our communities don't have the capacity to address all the other projects that are being thrown in our face at the same time. So we are trying to set the precedent that the federal government has to recognize Aboriginal rights and title, has to find a way to work with us where we can work together, because we all have to live here, and that the processes that are evaluating these projects are not undermining our sovereignty.

*So you see Enbridge as an important test case for other areas too?*

Yes, in setting the foundation for everything that our communities are experiencing with other projects, the lack of free prior informed consent, the lack of meaningful consultation, engagement.

*The duty to consult is required in theory, but are you saying that in practice that is mostly rhetoric?*

Yes, there's no teeth to it. It's just gums.

*As you say, Enbridge is this test case for other projects that might come along. How about pipelines that are* LNG *pipelines, are they proposed through your territory too?*

There are many natural gas pipelines being proposed. There's a lot of issues that are associated with those. Again, a lot of the communities don't have the capacity to assess a lot of the developments that are coming. There is still a lot of research that needs to be done, but there's also a lot of feelings around how even natural gas pipelines are fueling that tar sands beast. Like, with how they are extracting tar sands through open pit mining, but also fracking. They need a lot of fresh water. They need a lot of natural gas to heat up that water to inject it in the ground, just to get that bitumen out. But, it's energy suicide, so a lot of communities want free prior and informed consent, we still want to do our research. Of course, not all of our communities are against this development. We are experiencing rates of unemployment as high as 90 percent in some communities. Companies are preying on us because we don't have the capacity, and, not just our communities, but many communities in the north are looking for forms of employment. There's a lot of mixed feelings. Again, there's still a lot of research that needs to be done. There's still a lot of information that's not being shared in terms of the impacts that are associated with fracking.

*To this point, as I understand it, within the Yinka Dene Alliance, only the Wet'suwet'en has said no to* LNG *across their territory, but the other five have not taken a position as yet. Is that right?*

They haven't been as vocal. It's more an issue of where to prioritize our resources within our community, of which projects we are going to tackle first, and stating that Enbridge is the test case. But there are clans within the Wet'suwet'en Nation who have erected permanent cabins and camps along proposed oil and LNG pipeline routes within their territories.

*The province has come out against the Northern Gateway pipeline?*

It was a mini victory, I guess, to have the province say that they don't approve of this project going through. But, those five conditions that they have set still kind of leaves a toe in the door. We are not stupid. We are going to keep an eye on them as we have always done. And, again, use whatever means necessary to ensure that this project does not go through. And, this one project is the test case, in terms of other developments that may or may not happen here.

*The Yinka Dene Alliance is in many ways one of the most visible Northern Gateway opponents. You seem to not only have these very different and multiple levels of action, internationally and locally, but also make a very strong link between your own watershed issues and the tar sands production. Is the end goal to stop the tar sands, not just the pipeline?*

The rate of development is just so unsustainable. Just this one project alone, this Northern Gateway pipeline project, could increase tar sands development by 30 percent. That's one project. One pipeline. When Fort Chip has already experienced an increase in cancer rates. So, what would this one project do to communities like Fort Chipewyan?

*How has your alliance been able to be so successful in opposition compared to other communities? For example, would you say, that because 25 percent of the pipeline is going through your territory that it is of more importance to you than to other groups? Is it that you have more of a history or more capacity of organizing through other campaigns in the past that gives you that basis to build on? We are trying to understand why your group is at the forefront. Or perhaps it is particular individuals that have been radicalized or strengthened and empowered in the process?*

Let me tell you about my own family's personal history, in terms of direct action. My great-grandmother Sophie Thomas, the late Dr. Sophie Thomas, was an internationally renowned environmental activist but she was also a very traditional medicine woman as well. That is one of the gifts that is still present in our communities, that gift of healing, of treating many different people with cancers. When we hear about what is happening in the tar sands and seeing more increases of cancer, we know we have to keep those resources needed to heal our people. We know that there would be an oil spill. It's not if, it's when. What happens when we can't heal ourselves anymore? Within our community, there have been women from the Thomas family who have put a lot of dedication, a lot of time, a lot of sacrifice to this campaign. For us, for myself, it is important. I'm going to do it even if it means I'm hitchhiking around, I'm camping, I'm sleeping on someone's couch. It is so important that this project does not go through, and there are other members of my family who feel the same as well. Other communities here in the north know what my great-grandmother did in terms of environmental protection and fighting things such as clear-cut logging within our territory. We are also members of the Frog Clan. The Frog Clan are stewards of the water, and water is what gives everything life. And without healthy water our medicines will not have the power to heal anymore. Our communities will get sick. Our role is as stewards of the water, doing what we can to make sure that the veins of our Mother Earth are healthy, so that we can continue to be healthy and we can continue to live how we have always lived.

*It's very interesting that you said that it's the women who have played a leadership role. Is that something that perhaps characterizes the opposition?*

Yes.

*Is it beyond your own particular alliance? Are women more prominent generally, do you think?*

As I mentioned, being members of the Frog Clan, we are matrilineal, so everything is passed through the women, the knowledge, the power, the resources. A lot of responsibility goes through the women, but not just in the Yinka Dene Alliance communities but other First Nations communities who are also opposing these projects. It has been a lot of women; women from Fort Chipewyan, women from the Peace areas, women from American Indian tribes opposing these developments. Women are the givers of life, the caretakers. Our role and our duty as women is to step up because a lot of our communities are healing. A lot of people have lost their voices. A lot of men have lost their roles in the communities, but it is starting to revitalize. The women are standing up and the men are starting to come as well, and our communities are all being uplifted. When we did the Freedom Train across Canada to attend Enbridge's shareholder meeting in Toronto last year that was very major. We wanted to make that effort to stop at communities all along the way to have that person-to-person engagement to do ceremony with other communities. We all brought waters from our territories and all across Canada; we all mixed our waters together, and it's the water we are working for and praying for and doing whatever we can to keep healthy.

*One of the things that we've noticed with Enbridge is that interestingly they have sponsored a Women in Business event and now they are doing another event in Prince George later this month called Women Building Communities; it's about healthy eating or something. I'm just wondering if they are trying to build a community of women to oppose you. To find women who are supportive of the proposal. Do you see that happening? I'm just interested in why suddenly Enbridge is becoming interested in women.*

It's almost like they are mimicking our campaign. They have seen how effectively we have been able to make this such an international issue. They are trying to mimic it and to respond to how strong we have been in the media lately, and within social networks as well. They have started to amp up their media, their commercials, their radio ads.

*That must make you feel quite good, that you have them on the run?*

They are scared. They are so scared. We already feel that we have got this in the bag. In terms of their hopes and dreams of this project going through, they know it's not going to happen and they are scared. It's just one company, but there's all these other companies that are scared as well. If our Aboriginal rights and title aren't respected, cumulative impacts aren't acknowledged and free prior and informed consent isn't present, then the projects will not go ahead. Enbridge is one of the biggest pipeline companies in North America, and we have got them shaken. You talk about who's David and Goliath here!

*How important are connections with non-Aboriginal groups? Have you been able to bridge that gap?*

It has been so surreal in terms of the support that we have received from non-Aboriginals, and Canadians across the board. It's been great seeing all different generations as well, all different backgrounds. All coming together on this one issue and being so focused; it's unprecedented in our view. When we did the Freedom Train, stopping in different communities, at six in the morning we would stop somewhere. There's 200 people there, all different ages, ethnicities, whatever. They are bringing food from their gardens, bringing donations that they have fundraised, and that is the support that we've depended on and appreciate along this journey, is just from general Canadians across the board, who have supported us. And that's what has kept this momentum going.

*Have groups in the north, or in B.C., been particularly helpful to you?*

We have seen the B.C. Union of Municipalities pass different resolutions saying that they will not support this kind of unsustainable development. We have seen the City of Vancouver and different mayors actually proclaim Save the Fraser Declaration Day, and having this recognition regionally, domestically, it's been totally unreal. So, yes, a lot of different support from all different kinds of groups, NGOs, you name it, we have received incredible support.

*Have you been working with many NGOs?*

Oh yes, and it's been a learning process for our communities in terms of how NGOs work with our communities. We see a lot of the almost white knights, like we are going to come and we are going to save you and here's how you are going to do it. And it's like, whoa, whoa, whoa. And how we've addressed this is that we lead this movement. We speak for ourselves. You have to respect that, even as an NGO. Yes, you can be an ally, but we have got to have boundaries. We have got to have a good understanding of how we are going to work together that doesn't patronize us.

From day one we said that we would speak for ourselves and we are always seeking support and if NGOs want to support us, that's great. But, we are leading this. We are doing this and they have to respect that. But the media has been trying to put that out there that we are just little puppets of outside NGOs. I don't think so!

*Sometimes you get celebrities who come in and bless campaigns. Does that help you or does it just give the opposition some fodder?*

Any support that we receive is helpful. We have had celebrities offer their support as well, and if they can use their outreach through their fame, their access to the media, then so be it. I think it's pretty well known that our communities have been the lead in the opposition to this pipeline project. And we are going to receive support from anywhere right now.

*What other Aboriginal groups have been in the forefront with the Yinka Dene Alliance?*

The Coastal First Nations are very strong players. They really inspired the Yinka Dene Alliance in terms of the Save the Fraser Declaration that they put out. I think from there, communities just started to realize that, in terms of a legal means we are going to use, we are going to use Indigenous laws as well. I think communities along the coast, but also our communities here in the interior, have been very strong. But, also right in the tar sands too. I think that's where I started to feel inspired, in the roles that communities have taken in the tar sands regions, how they have been working to address these developments in their territories. A lot of working together has been important.

*Now, it's clear that Enbridge is running scared. I suppose the federal government must be running scared as well.*

Oh, they are so running scared. You have seen the recent cuts to environmental protection? It's a result, a direct result from this project, and we see that the federal government, how buddy-buddy they are with this particular company and the changes that they will make to environmental protection. It's pretty evident that they are scared as well, and especially with this movement growing around Idle No More, which started off from those cuts they made to environmental protection. They are very scared right now.

*Who ultimately do you think has to be convinced to stop this? Is it the company? Is it the federal government? Is it communities on the route? From your perspective, when you are campaigning who is the target that has to be stopped?*

I think it's a lot to do with the federal government. There's a lot of First Nations who are pretty pissed off in terms of how they deal with our communities, with these development projects. The companies, it doesn't matter which one, they are all about the money. They are not going to stop for anything. If they are friends with the federal government they will make the necessary changes they think that will help that project to proceed.

*But do you think the federal government would, or do you think that they can, proceed against this united resistance?*

I think they are going to try to use the national interest argument until they are blue in the face. The international community could put more pressure on Canada in terms of its energy policies and everything like that.

*The problem with this particular government is that it's not likely to respond to interna-tional pressures. They don't seem to care one bit. I think their big problem is the strong legal position that you have, your territorial rights.*

There's different groups who are taking that path through to court right now, like in Alberta and along the coast here, and challenging the FIPA with China. In terms of treaty violations in Alberta, the Beaver Lake Cree are also going through the court system as well, which could really have an impact on the growth of the tar sands. Those paths are being pursued and it could interfere with the agenda to have more trade with Asia.

*You only need one of those legal challenges to have some legs and it can tie it all up. And, of course, that could be for years and years. You mentioned that you had met with groups in South America too. I was just wondering which groups you had met with and how you met with them?*

I had the opportunity to attend the World Peoples Conference on Climate Change and for the Protection of Mother Earth. I was in Cochabamba, Bolivia, with 30,000 plus other people, discussing how our Indigenous peoples are going to address this climate crisis, and then all collectively fighting for that basic principle of free prior and informed consent, which is the cornerstone for our movement.

*How has free prior and informed consent worked in practice?*

It's been very frustrating. Very overwhelming, because, anybody can go online and stick a claim in our territory and there's no consultation, meaningful engage-ment whatsoever. It's just exploding. Again, trying to find the resources, having a capacity to address all of these other projects happening has been overwhelming. It's the wild wild west over here, that's what it feels like.

*In the federal government's fight back to this resistance, do they ever throw out this notion of corporate social responsibility to say that a company should be allowed to proceed as long as they meet corporate social responsibility criteria?*

Yes, and they are also saying if you have concerns then bring them to the Joint Review Panel. Bring it to that table. And we are saying no, we are not going to sit at that table. That process doesn't respect anything about us. They are going to take this and try to portray it as we don't care, that we have no concerns.

*You seem to have been able to forge links and have the degree of solidarity, which is very impressive and very enviable. How have you been able to do that? Is it because of historic links within the communities that you think your understanding, your clarity in addressing this whole issue, makes it possible?*

I think so. The history within our family and our communities here has been a big part of it. But, also the solidarity aspect that you mentioned. Understanding that we can't do this alone. We have had a lot of support from the Indigenous Environmental Network, who are really well known for their work in the international community in terms of Indigenous rights and pushing for that. So, again, seeking support and guidance from people who have great experience running international campaigns. They have sought out a lot of support, and we did our research.

*When you say, "we did our research," do you have a research office?*

Like where is the major anti-Enbridge headquarters?! It's been three of us, four of us women sitting in a living room one night and saying, "Hey, let's do a train across the country." Or camping out on the land and saying, "Hey, let's go do this." And it's been just very grassroots, women sitting around the coffee table, thinking how are we going to do this?

*Do you go on the internet and look at all the scientific reports and evidence?*

Yes, we are keeping up to date with that as much as we can. And, sharing resources with other communities as well and making sure that we are all going in the right direction together because we can't do it alone, individually.

*In this process of getting together, is that just through meetings and encounters? Or do you rely on social media or electronic communication?*

Social media has been huge, which is, I think, a big part of how we have been so successful in getting our message out because the media will block out a lot of stuff. But, a lot of people depend on social media for their information nowadays. Our communities are primarily within the ages of thirty and under, and in 75 percent of our communities, 50 percent at least is in that age group, and they rely on social media. A lot of Facebook, Twitter and Instagram, sharing photos. Like, this is what my land means to me and different campaigns like that of culturalization in a way, but using these new tools and these new weapons basically.

*So, this has been a movement with youth being engaged as well?*

I think my generation, I am twenty-six years old, and I think our generation has seen a lot of our parents and their parents were almost too quiet for a long time. Because of those impacts from residential school and you are going to do what you're told and don't talk back, and be the good little Indian men. I think, growing up seeing that, a lot of youth have found their voice, which has also uplifted the voices of those who have been impacted by colonization as well. So, it's like a healing journey together, where our voices are coming through more strongly now.

*Well, I almost feel sorry for Enbridge, what they are up against. They also have the Northern Gateway Alliance.*

That was so funny. After the Yinka Dene Alliance was formed, then, again, the mimicking. Oh, the Northern Gateway Alliance and, oh, the Women's Group. We almost think it's pretty humorous to see how scared they are and how they are seeing the strengths of our campaign and our tactics. They are trying to use it and thinking they are going to get the same results. But, it's a joke.

*What other activities have you been involved in?*

I did attend the Bank of Nova Scotia's AGM there, and my experience with that was just unreal. One of the shareholders actually got up and made some very racist remarks. I actually received an apology from the bank, which surprised me, like "Sorry for the response that came from one of the shareholders that was there. We are sorry that that happened."

*Just thinking again about this, you work locally, regionally, nationally and internationally. Is there a level at which it's more important to work at than others, in terms of affecting and getting the result you want? Or, does it just depend on circumstances?*

Circumstances. I think this whole pipeline project, it has almost in a way been good for our communities in the sense that it has brought so many people together to have a unified voice on one single issue has been major. So, locally, starting to get people more aware of that water that we still depend on today, that when we go to the land, it's going to be impacted. And bringing that awareness around a people, it really opens a lot in terms of what it is at stake here, seeing it. Like, it's right there. That river. That water body is going to be impacted. And then having a good base of local awareness on this issue, it just grows.

*The federal government, in its support of mining companies in Peru and Bolivia, have funded and launched faith-based NGOs like Vision Canada. Would they do that here? Have a faith-based NGO to intervene on behalf of the company or the government?*

I haven't really seen the company really try to get faith-based organizations to help them. We have seen faith-based organizations ask how they could support us, and what they could do, and they have. They have collected donations, which help our campaign. But we have had a lot of attacks from the government through the media that we are 'eco-terrorists'. They are trying to put that really negative slant on how we are resisting. Like we are terrorists — and it's women, it's children, it's grandmothers.

Rick Mercer did a skit on it about the announcement of terrorists and he actually used a picture of me as their image of the terrorist, and it's just me in my regalia; like this is a terrorist, right? I've also been featured in the CBC's documentary series, the 8*th* *Fire* as well. So, I was just one of the voices, one of the youth voices in this country. I think it's been inspiring for a lot of our community members that we have the right to say no to what happens in our territory. Again, we are not opposed to everything, but on this one particular project, having someone as young as myself, I think it had an effect on other youth within my generation as well, who were also finding that voice. But seeing that image of terrorists that the government is pushing through the media, the problems that I see with that is that I don't want that image to reflect the work that we are doing. We endorse peaceful, non-violent, direction action, and I think having the government trying to portray us crazy, just extremists, is wrong. I would never want the image of myself, and what I do, to be ever reflected in the way that they want it to be.

# ~ John Phair ~

*John Phair lives in the community of Burns Lake, a municipality with approximately 3,600 people. John moved there in 2002 to be closer to his family and to offer landscaping consultation; he now works at the local College. Before that he lived in Ontario, where he was born. He studied music at Queens University, was a professional church musician for thirty years (in Ottawa, Peterborough and Toronto), was the purchasing manager at the Royal Conservatory Music Store (then affiliated with University of Toronto) and has worked with a small organ builder and component supplier. He was a communications officer for Epilepsy Ontario for seven years. As well as his love of music he has always been keen to help when he sees injustice. He is now a member of the Lakes District Clean Water Coalition, formed out of concern over the Enbridge project.*

*We talked with John in the living room of his house in Burns Lake. He spoke to us in a personal capacity not as a spokesperson for the Coalition.*

---

*John, I imagine that in your day job, as a facilitator at the college here, you must see a lot of emphasis on energy-related trades training.*

In terms of students at the college, I believe it must be approaching 80 percent First Nations. Currently, some of them are in support programs for training for office work and things like food preparation. But the majority of them right now are being retrained for the trades: digging out corridors for energy, even though I suspect that they realize they won't get jobs in those fields anyway. But they have no options in terms of funding: if they want to be funded for further education, that's what's open to them.

I feel that I have to watch what I say publically in terms of the college. Most of the programs at the local college are run on a cost-recovery basis. So if you don't have students, it closes down.

*Are the First Nations part of the Yinka Dene Alliance, which has taken the very strong position against the Enbridge pipeline?*

Yes, the Yinka Dene have certainly spoken against the Enbridge pipeline. There's fractionalization or disruption within communities and between communities as I see it, especially around the LNG Pacific Trail pipeline (PTP). The position of the Wet'suwet'en peoples is absolutely no way to oil or gas pipelines. I personally feel they're on the right track. People are slow to see what's happening here. You have just come through the village and see how the

40

roads are narrowed and so on. How are they going to cope with quadrupling the truck traffic?

*Why would they narrow the roads?*

To beautify the downtown. It's a part of the revitalization of the downtown. I've already heard of at least two that I can remember, where large trucks have had to stop and back up on the highway because they took the corners too sharply and can't get around.

*Apart from the increased traffic, what are the arguments here against pipelines?*

One of the arguments against is that once one pipeline goes through, I've heard from some sources that they are already aware of fourteen pipelines that they are talking of pushing through there. Another thing that people are starting to become aware of is that even though a pipeline may be slated as a gas pipeline, it could be converted to something else later. And people are starting, especially amongst the First Nations, to be aware of how other countries might covet Lake Babine or Francois Lake for its water.

*Can you elaborate on that?*

Well, given the changes that are happening in the global climate and the shortages of water that are happening in, certainly in China and also in the States, in California, the bread basket or the food basket there, it wouldn't be that difficult to reconfigure a natural gas or even a dilbit (diluted bitumen) pipeline to transport water. And Lake Babine is just twenty minutes away from here. And Francoise Lake is only twenty minutes, half an hour south of here. They're both quite huge.

*You certainly live in a water-rich area. Could you tell us about your group?*

Lakes District Clean Water Coalition started in the fall of 2010 mainly out of concern about the Enbridge pipeline and looking at Enbridge's history, and from my perspective, looking at the tar sands. There are about a dozen people in the Coalition who are really keenly active, and a core of about thirty to thirty-five who come out to many of the public events and showings and discussions. The mailing list is about 130 now. We're part of the coalitional groups from Prince George to Prince Rupert that keep each other informed about what's going on.

*As a coalition, does it work as an information exchange or more than that?*

It's mainly information exchange. There's some working together in terms of providing us print material which we otherwise could not afford, allowing us opportunities to join in larger movements, such as the event going on in Terrace next week.

*How do you work with the Yinka Dene Alliance?*

I know a number of the people in the Alliance, and we communicate about what's going on locally. They're on our mailing list, and they let me know if things are happening. At the big meeting that occurred two years ago, we were invited to participate in that. Information exchange is the biggest thing right now.

*What do you see as the main obstacles to building a deeper relationship?*

There's division amongst the First Nations and within the First Nations, and the governments are just pitting one against the other, and pitting family member against family member. I personally fluctuate between being very sad and being very angry, especially when remembering the police raid of the Ts'il Kaz Koh community centre in April.

*Where would the pipeline go?*

In terms of local communities here, the pipelines would go through Burns Lake Band and Wet'suwet'en territory, and would cut right along the Lake Babine Nation reserve here. The proposed pipeline route has what amounts to a 90 degree turn just west of the proposed pumping station. And the lay of the land, according to Enbridge's maps, shows that any potential leaks there would come right into Saul Creek which is a hundred metres the other side of Fifth Avenue here. [In places, Saul Creek is as close as twenty metres from homes along Sixth Avenue.] The creek goes right down past the college into Burns Lake, not far from where the Burns Lake Band gets its water.

When the Enbridge squad was here in August, our group was there, Lakes District Clean Waters Coalition, and we refused to go into the meeting building.

*They were holding hearings?*

This was an information session. At that point, when we refused to go in and there were as many of us outside as there were people inside, they came out to speak with us. When I asked them specifically about the pressures in the pipes at the outlet of the pumping stations and recounted that I had read in their documentation to the JRP that it could be in the range of 2,600 PSI coming out of the pumping station, they wouldn't dismiss that. They wouldn't confirm or deny anything.

*Has the mayor and council taken any position on Enbridge?*

No, they've categorically refused to. We asked for two years for them to have public hearings. There was an opportunity to have a public forum organized by some folks from UNBC. But Enbridge refused to participate in that, so UNBC had no option but to cancel it.

*So your group has held events and showings of movies have you?*

Yes, we've had our presence at the fair for the last couple years. We've had a number of movies overlapping with a couple of other groups here. With the local Idle No More group, we've had a showing of *Occupy Love,* which was more well attended than I anticipated. We were trying to have a showing of the newest one, *Do the Math,* from 350.org. Because people are so busy, and as soon as the snow goes, everybody's gone, we're now distributing discs with the movies on them.

*So that's your main sort of activities, to try and get information out to the public?*

At this point, yes, and trying to participate with other groups to continue the discussion. One of the last things that we did was to take a map from Enbridge's website showing the proposed route and looked at the American data that showed that in many cases with a spill, they evacuate a mile on each side of the spill. So I drew, on the map, a mile in each direction, and a mile up from the water frontage once it hits the lake and rivers, and we published that — just a flyer that was going out to people who go to one of the health food stores or various other places. It was also shown at the fair as well.

*What forms of communication do you mostly use?*

I use Facebook quite frequently, and email, to deal with the issues around pipelines, energy, mining and human rights. We also post information about when we're meeting and if it's a public meeting, for business and so on, information as well specifically about human rights abuses that are going on. One of my personal concerns is what's happening with the mining sector in South America. A few women from Lake Babine Nation are very active with First Nations Women Advocating Responsible Mining.

*There's organized resistance to mines in countries such as Peru and Ecuador, indeed everywhere. So there's some reaching into northern British Columbia as well then.*

Yes, and there's the history here for the people here to touch on as well because of what happened with the Cheslatta Carrier Nation peoples south of here when, in the 1950s, Alcan built the huge Nechako reservoir, which changed the direction of the water flow and started diverting water to Kemano. It totally flooded the area. I know of people who came home from hunting and found that their village had been flooded out. They didn't know where any of their family was. They came across to Burns Lake on foot. Some of them were paid fifty dollars each for their loss. The same sort of thing has happened and is going on, still going on at Amazay with the Tse Keh Nay people at Duncan Lake. So people have that in their active memory. As someone from Ontario, I was astounded, we are taught so little about Aboriginal history. People my age are amongst the people who were relocated to Burns Lake Band reserves and to Lake Babine Nation reserves — torn off of the lake and brought down to the reserve here, miles away from it on the other side of the watershed. And given fifty dollars.

*Since then the court rulings seemed to have given a lot more power to Aboriginal peoples in terms of their ability to fight projects such as Enbridge. Would you say that's the case?*

Yes. but my own personal feeling is that the federal government has determined it's going to push ahead no matter what. I also think that Enbridge was made the test case to deflect attention away from the gas pipeline just south of here, the PTP pipeline.

*An interesting strategy because with concern over heavy oil, gas looks relatively harmless.*

Yes, it seems innocuous. We have one gas line running north of here already which has exploded, but it's relatively innocuous. Mercifully there was no fire. But again, there's been deception about how clean that gas is, looking at its carbon footprint from fracking through to burning. And so consequently the nations south of here have signed on for the PTP pipeline, even though their people are against it.

*Your coalition, the Lakes Coalition, what is your objective now?*

Our ongoing objective is to bring information to people about all of these related issues and to encourage people to do what they feel is appropriate for them to do, to take action against these pipelines: whether that's appealing to the MLA and the local councils, whether that's talking with people locally, whether that's participating in rallies here or elsewhere, or whether that's more than that.

*And so a successful outcome for you would be no Enbridge and no gas pipelines?*

Yes, at this point in time. We get accused of being anti-development, but no, it just has to be development that's not raping the Earth.

*I'm just trying to get a sense of whether your campaign is a localized issue around pipelines or whether it's actually the tar sands and fracking that are the objectives.*

The local. There is discussion in the local group about that and there's no strong consensus. I think the bulk of the people who are involved more often see this local stuff as part of the global, that the tar sands and fracking are both not acceptable. But then there's other people who are more conciliatory and see the very real fact that no matter what the outcome is, we all have to still live here. Nevertheless, if we don't stop the tar sands, nobody's going to be living here, in twenty years or forty years. Nobody's going to be living here anyway because it won't be a habitable climate.

*Have the churches played a role?*

Other than what the United Church has done publically, there's been nothing locally amongst the churches that I've been aware of. At the March Against Monsanto a couple weeks ago, the pastor of one of the congregations joined us. I was glad to see him.

*Have there been any international environmental NGOs that have played a role?*

The most prominent group would have been the group from the U.N., the Nobel Women's Initiative [who visited in October 2012].

*Have you linked up with the opposition groups to Keystone in the U.S.?*

There was some discussion of that early in the spring, if Keystone is success-fully delayed or even stopped, about moving their attention to B.C. But I wonder whether that would be fragmented because of the proposed route through here and the proposed expansion of Kinder Morgan. There's a lot more people to fight the Kinder Morgan one than there are here. But in all truth, there are people here, both Indigenous and newcomers, who would be prepared to stand against the pipeline.

*I know Maude Barlow from the Council of Canadians was out west and she talked at UNBC, and was trying to put a national dimension to the opposition.*

We have had some amazing people come through here. Riki Ott spoke here, and Beth Wallace, National Wildlife Federation from Battle Creek Michigan, and Erin O'Brien, Wisconsin Wetlands, were here in December 2010.

The turnout for Riki Ott was on a beautiful Saturday morning with not much notice, so we had twenty-five or thirty people for that. Mind you, that was all that showed up for the last Enbridge event, as well as when Patrick Moore was through here too. It was a small group of mainly his supporters. Actually it may have been enlightening for them, because he sat in a room at the college which was fifteen metres away from Saul Creek, through which the pipeline would drain if there were a leak in the region, and talked about the pipeline being "out in the booneys." He actually got boos at that point.

*So who brought Patrick Moore through? Who sponsored him?*

That was Enbridge.

*Did you make a submission to the JRP?*

I signed up on behalf of Lakes District Clean Waters Coalition as an intervener, mainly to be kept in the loop and have access to all the documentation. I decided very early that the whole thing was a sham!

I made an oral presentation in July 2012, when the JRP was here in Burns Lake. Altogether, fifteen local people presented, all in opposition to the proposed NGP project.

*Has the Northern Gateway Alliance been around?*

Oh yes, oh yes.

*Do they do public speaking or just speak with the Chamber of Commerce?*

Mainly the latter sort of things now. And many of those aren't made public anymore. Our group objected regularly about all the meetings of Enbridge and its minions. We objected in the newspaper as well, because nobody was informed about these meetings beforehand while we were asking the village council to either have a public debate or to allow more than a six-minute "Committee of the Whole" meeting for us to present.

*So now you have given up with the village council, where do you see your main attention being, who are you trying to influence now? Is it the province, the company, the local governments?*

Individuals. I think individuals are our main focus, until the governments actually see how many people are opposed. That means getting people out on a Saturday morning to stomp around in public and show that there are people who are opposed to this, or at least question this. Some people figure that the First Nations will take care of it and stop it all. And that attitude just makes me crazy.

*So what's your best guess? Is the federal government going to ram it through regardless of all of this resistance and opposition?*

My fear is that they will try to ram it through. If not directly the current Enbridge proposal, wait for a few years and tag it onto the PTP proposal. But either way, I don't see any pipelines being built without confrontation. I really fear there will be blood shed over it. It makes me sick to my stomach to think of that. But I don't see how, there are enough First Nations people who are pissed off enough and trust the governments so little, especially given the international status of these territories, in terms of being unceded.

*And the stakes are so high. This government will probably force opponents into violent confrontations because they will probably not be given an alternative.*

It looks like they're setting a stage for that to me. You can see that from the fact that fifty police officers, including snipers, were sent to evict a couple adults and kids on a Sunday morning.

# ~ John Ridsdale ~

*John Ridsdale is a member of the Tsayu (Beaver) Clan, House of Tsa K'ex Yex. He lives in Tse Kya (Hagwilget) and works in Smithers at the Office of the Wet'suwet'en Natural Resources Department. Since becoming a member of the Office of the Wet'suwet'en team, he has taken on the responsibility of carrying the hereditary chief name of Na'Moks, Chief of the Tsayu Clan, a name he does not carry lightly, as there are roles and responsibilities that must be fulfilled above all others. The main portion of his duties is to ensure that the land of the Wet'suwet'en is taken care of in a manner that is consistent with Wet'suwet'en values and traditions, following Wet'suwet'en laws regarding protection of land, people, culture and the Feast Hall, as this is their House of Parliament and place of worship.*

*In his role as resource referral coordinator, John coordinates the Wet'suwet'en response to resource development proposals on their territory. The Office of the Wet'suwet'en exercises governance over the management of resources within their territory; the referral assessment process is of importance to provide better decision-making information to communities and maintain Wet'suwet'en cultural identity. He also sits on the Wet'suwet'en Unlocking Aboriginal Justice Advisory Board, Child Welfare Advisory Board and the Office of the Wet'suwet'en Executive Committee. His educational background includes studies in environmental stewardship, governance, sociology and business administration.*

*John's interests include hunting, history and culture.*

*We met with John at the Office of the Wet'suwet'un in Smithers. Before we started the interview, John showed around the office, including the boardroom, which contains the table used at the Delgamuukw negotiations. The Wet'suwet'un had requested the table as a lasting reminder of their victory. For the interview, we went to the library, a room crammed with documents relating to the case.*

---

*John, could you start by telling us about how you first became involved as the pipeline point person for the Wet'suwet'en Chiefs.*

First off, I'm a natural resources coordinator. I'm employed at the Office of the Wet'suwet'en in the Natural Resource Department. But I'm also a hereditary chief, Na'Moks. I'm currently the highest-ranking chief with the Tsayu Clan, the Beaver Clan. I am one of the younger chiefs, and you have to realize that, for every proposed pipeline, there are in excess of 20,000 documents. So we have to go through them all and decide what is the important information to present to our elders. We have an environmental assessment coordinator and that's his specific duty, strictly looking at these pipeline proposals. That's his entire duty in this office. I coordinate the clans, we meet with them, we update them. Number one, these are only proposed pipelines. The nation itself has already stated they will not come across our territory because they'll split the territory in half, and no matter what it is, whether it's oil, condensate or natural gas, the fact is, the construction of it totally splits our territory in half. And during the construction, we are starting to realize they have to pressure test the pipes. So, they have got to get that water from somewhere, pressurize it, put it in the pipes and then they have got to dispose of it. Now that's dead water.

*Did the Enbridge proposal address these issues?*

No, they're going as simplistic as possible and that's why I think that even the Joint Review Panel has to look at it as incomplete reports. When Enbridge first came here they said they are here for a pipeline and nothing to do with tankers. They just wanted to make it as simplistic and as site specific as possible. And it was ourselves that were the first ones to get up and tell them: you're not just talking about a pipeline, you're talking about a pipeline corridor. Pacific Trails pipeline, the same thing. There is now one natural gas pipeline. It's a nine-inch pipeline that was put in in the 1960s before we completed the Delgamuukw/Gisdaywa court case. So we didn't have much of a say in that. Now they even want to expand that, where we do have a say now. But when they use the word pipeline and they use the word corridor, those are two separate animals. One is basically a back road and the other is a freeway. I believe sixteen First Nations have signed on to the Pacific Trails pipeline. They called it a First Nations limited partnership. The Wet'suwet'en are the only ones that wouldn't join it because they had a corridor in there.

And they didn't go into the other aspects of construction, what they're going to haul, what laws will be followed and which ones would be changed. Prime Minister Harper, with his omnibus bills, has proven us right. When you get an omnibus bill that stops protection what do you get? You get 99.7 percent of lakes not protected. That's exactly what we have now but our law, or traditional law, is higher than the province of B.C. and the federal government. We believe they're going against our laws and the constitution of Canada. That's why on the 20th of last month, as Na'Moks, I held a feast and in that feast banned all pipelines. We have five clans in the Wet'suwet'en Nation, and the other four will follow suit and host their own feasts to support this decision. That is the communal decision and that's what democracy is, our people say what they decide and the chiefs follow through with the decision. The people decide.

*How does the federal government react to this?*

Their law is not nearly as old as our law. Each court case we look at, and there's in excess of sixty court cases in the last four or five years, not one of them has been in favour of the government because they pushed the boundaries.

*So the federal government is not following its own laws?*

Their own law that they've established themselves and they'll refer to it, but it doesn't mean they always follow it. This is an ongoing issue.

Last Thursday David Black [who has proposed an oil refinery at the Enbridge pipeline terminus in Kitimat] was at the First Nations Summit. I saw going through the crowd, there's 200 to 300 of us chiefs there. So he was picking and choosing elected chiefs and elected councillors, and they were going into a side meeting. There are six reserves on our territory so I'd say four of them have come and asked, "Are you a part of this meeting?" I said, "I haven't been invited." They said, "Well we're not going, we only have jurisdiction on a reserve." Hereditary chiefs, we have jurisdiction on the land. And so they said they'll give up their seat and that I needed to be in there, so I attended the meeting. And his proposal is exactly like Enbridge's. And he was picking and choosing who he would speak to, you know, the path of least resistance. "Here's some money. We know you're living on a reserve. We know you need health and education, housing because you're being starved out, so come to this meeting."

And they know that the leadership, that the Wet'suwet'en hereditary leadership, will never give up our authority on the land. So they said, "Well, you better talk to the hereditary leadership because they represent the entire nation, not just the village." So that's where I went in there and just told them exactly what I thought as did other chiefs. Some of the other ones got up and left and said, "This is for the hereditary chiefs and it's got nothing to do with the reserve." And that's finally sinking in, these agreements that Enbridge said they have, they won't tell us who has signed on. But they understand that the truth already lies with the people and the nation. I think that's where industry doesn't get it; it's a foreign concept to them. They won't understand and they won't try to understand.

*The band leaders are, I suppose, an easier group to identify and perhaps entice?*

They're elected to represent our reserve, to make that reserve healthier and better within the reserve boundary. But within two or three years, there's another election, will they still be there? Or won't they still be there? Whereas with hereditary chiefs, when I pass away, there's already another person that is chosen to pick up that name. The name will always remain just us as people, as humans, we change. But it's the duty of the chief to make sure that the next one that carries on that name is fully trained and fully understands the duties that come with it.

It's far more than a job. It has to be, simply, a way of life, of belief. So that's what chiefs mean about the protection of the land, the connection to the land, and the spirituality that goes with it.

They have a great saying: if we don't speak for the animals, the fish and the birds, who will? Simple, very simple, very to the point. And how could we give up something that our great-great-grandchildren will ask us one day 'Why don't we have this anymore? Why didn't you stop this then?' We don't have a right to let that happen. The Gitxsan, Wet'suwet'en and Gitanyow are unique in all of Canada because of the Delgamuukw/Gisdaywa court case and the fact that we are led by hereditary leadership. Which is why we are Enbridge's strongest opponent, I believe, against pipelines.

*So the pipelines themselves, when you say they would divide between north and south, you mean they would physically cut a corridor through your territory?*

Yes, they have to have a buffer for each pipeline for liability reasons. They have private roads that travel long distances. This is for their maintenance and they can't let the public on that. So you can't go across it; it's a liability issue.

*That does effectively divide your territory. They would have to have fences that are private property across your territory?*

They claim it won't, but I've already made the visits up to where these things happen and you don't have access to get in there, whereas right now we have free access to moose, berries, plants. Wherever we want to go, we have access. The roads that are on the territory right now cover a lot of our trails, but even that access will be restricted too. It has to be for liability reasons and the public fully hasn't been addressed on that one.

*This is something quite new. Most people talk about the threat of spills but you are talking about physical barriers on the land.*

They claim right now that they we won't restrict us, but I've already seen what they've done. I've been to the tar sands. I've been to Fort McMurray. I've been to Fort McKay. I've been to Fort St. John, just to have a look at the difference between oil, gas and the tar sands itself, and when we were up there, I think last time I was up at tar sands was last July, they actually had restricted air space, where you can't go over the industrial plants. Okay here's your flight pattern and you have to go around them. And I always thought that was only over military installations, but it's actually over the plants in the tar sands, there's no fly zones.

*Why would that be? Are they afraid someone might bomb it or something?*

I think they realize right now it's the second largest oil producer in the world and so if someone really wants to cripple the economy, that's it, and they won't make that public. I'm not a conspiracy theorist, but I always thought it was only military installations that you could not go over.

When we were up there, I've never ever stepped on such dead ground before. I talked to the elders and they can't swim in their lakes anymore, they won't drink the water, the berries don't even grow, they don't bloom anymore, just from the toxicity of the air. And you know it's funny because we were sitting there and there were about ten or twelve of us up there, and we were meeting with the elders and we were sitting around there and we were sharing a lunch and they put berries on the table and I just pushed them away. "Oh don't worry about it, we flew those in" they said.

I don't want that for our people. My freezer has moose meat in it, it has salmon, a smokehouse that we work every year. Our berries, we share them in our Feast Hall, that's part of our culture. We stand and hold the berries up in a bowl. One person will drum and he'll sing and he'll dance. That's just an acknowledgement that the berries come from the territory and we're sharing them. I can't believe that something would affect us so badly that parts of our culture would have to change severely.

*Have you ever had a conversation with either people in the government or in Enbridge about this?*

I think it's beyond their comprehension. They want to talk strictly on the sciences, and they'll always try to bring the conversation back to the monetary value. It's almost like they want to put a price tag on our culture, on our people, on our history, our language, our land.

*They probably do.*

And we won't quantify that for them, we're not going to make it easy for them. We've given them other, less damaging options, such as staying away from the watersheds, because you have to give options. But they've never, ever listened; it's all about the almighty dollar. There's more money saved if you go in a straight line but you have to realize that from Alberta to Kitimat there are in excess of 700 creeks, rivers and streams; that's a lot to damage.

*Have you actually proposed options? Alternatives?*

Yes, but it requires not crossing major waterways. It's inconceivable to me that you would threaten two of the largest rivers in British Columbia, two of the highest salmon producers in British Columbia, for pipelines, which are doing no good to Canada, other than taxes. That's it. It's not staying in Canada; it's all getting shipped overseas.

*What if they finally listened to you and involved you in the decision-making process, to find a way out, to find a way through your territory, would that be possible at this point? Or is it beyond that now?*

They've never taken it seriously and that's the problem. So it's much easier to have a provincial and federal government change the policy and legislation than it is to actually adapt to where a communication level can start. It's almost like they are saying, "We're doing this regardless." Well, now they have found out through the courts that it's not regardless. You know the strongest opposition are the First Nations. Each year I get sent to Enbridge's AGMs with their investors. So I simply tell them the truth: the last time we went to court, in excess of twenty years were tied up. Are you going to sit on your money for twenty years? Well, of course, they don't want to hear that because they're there to make money. They're not going to sit on money for twenty years. So it's starting to dawn on them: we aren't just an inconvenience. That's the way the government looks at us, they only look at us as an inconvenience until we go to court. We're just a nuisance level at this point. But it's when we get to the next stage. They're starting to realize constitutionally they can't do it. They can't ignore us because of the connection that we have to the land.

It's finally dawning on them. We're not some South American country where if they wipe out a tribe or a village, nobody cares. Because you've seen that. And we told them that they were on the world stage and made them think. I am the son of a Second World War veteran. He was there for the entire years that Canada was in the Second World War, seven ships shot out from under him. And now his son, his children, his grandchildren, his great grandchildren are being told that they don't have a voice in their own country. You don't exist because, even with court cases behind you, it's the almighty dollar that counts. He'd roll over in his grave. I know he would because this is not what he went to war for and this is not what we were raised for. We were raised to look after the land, the water, and whether industry believes it or not, we're not against industry. But if you do it right we will work with you. Right now pipelines are not willing to do it and it's not about the money. They've offered us an amount of money that would make your head spin. And it's not about the money because they're making us quantify it. What is this river worth? What is that creek worth? What is a salmon worth? What is a medicinal plant worth? That's what they want to quantify, and to me, there cannot be a monetary value put it. There simply cannot.

*Do they think that at some point you will just accept?*

They'll have to come to realize that you can't do it unless you have the social licence. Right now I think that they think it's just business as usual. "We've had a discussion. Here's some money. Here's a signature. Let's move on, next project." And they're finding out that's just not the way it is in British Columbia. Last year,

I went across Canada in what we called the Freedom Train as part of the Yinka Dene Alliance. The farther east we got, the more obvious it became to us that the faith in the democracy of Canada is waning so badly. But we are in a democratic country and we asked people, "Why are you not raising your voices?" Then when the Idle No More movement started up that really helped because that was the women and children leading that. And they were telling us, number one, we want to be peaceful. We do.

The fact is that they keep asking us constantly in the media, "how far are you willing to go to protect your land, your culture, your future?" My only answer is how far is Enbridge willing to go to force us? Why are these questions even being asked to us? The answer should still be with the corporations and the government; we shouldn't be forced to answer those questions. As I said, I have been to a number of Enbridge AGMs and I can't help but remind them that you billionaires are so poor. All you have is money. That's all you have, you know? You two guys are now in Smithers. Look how beautiful this is. Can you put a monetary value on that? On clean air, drinking clean water, being out able to relax and enjoy nature. It's not a hard question to answer; you just have to take the time and take a breath, that's all.

*How did you get to go to the AGMs, did they invite you?*

No, you actually have to be an investor, so we found people that have a limited amount of shares and so I get a proxy and I go. And they allow you two minutes at the microphone, so after two minutes I just cycle around to go back to microphone, two more minutes, cycle around and go back to the microphone. Make sure that you give yourself enough time to ask the questions that you want on the record and then — you'll never get a decent answer I don't believe — they'll refer you to an engineer department.

*Do you think the provincial government is jumping the gun with this newly created Ministry of Natural Gas? The government wants B.C. to be debt free, so they've a lot riding on this, haven't they? Even though they've come out against Enbridge, they've pinned a lot on LNG.*

But isn't it up to the public of British Columbia and the First Nations to have the final say? I often say it should not be an elected official that makes a decision; you should go to the people. That's why I constantly say that true democracy in British Columbia and Canada is being threatened because there's a limited amount of people that are making decisions for the entirety, without the permission of the people. We have to remind our Canadian people that if you don't raise your hand, speak what you think, it's almost like you're giving them permission to go ahead with it. And the propaganda they got out there, newspaper, TV, radio, "Oh, it's going to cure all the problems we'll ever have." No, this is just a Band-Aid solution and it's going to become worse. So why not just take your time, find out exactly what's going on?

Canada will not fall apart. Canada has a future and has a bigger and stronger future. Don't leave it up to a limited amount of people; everybody should have a voice in it. People from all over the world come here just to enjoy what we have, and yet, our democracy is going downhill. It just amazes me that we have people that come from some very, very, very terrible countries, where human rights atrocities have happened and the reason why they come to Canada is to enjoy freedom. And here we are allowing Steven Harper to sign a FIPA agreement which is going to be in effect for thirty-one years and we can get sued if we turn down the Chinese on the deal. We never had anything to say about that. On Wednesday, I was in Vancouver and I went to the FIPA protest they had because Port Alberni has taken the federal government to court over that agreement. Wednesday was their first day in court. I was down there for that and it's amazing that very little was said about this. Port Alberni's not the hugest place in Canada, but still to have the courage to take on the federal government over an international deal on behalf of all Canadians. I thought, "I need to be here."

*What about the natural gas pipeline?*

Our elders say that we're all related, so I often think — not only with the fracking, but with the construction on our territory — what happens? They say if the gas leaks it will evaporate. Nothing truly evaporates, never. It doesn't disappear just because you don't see it. And again with the propaganda they're using, it's almost like we're going to fade away if we don't develop natural gas. Well, no, we're not going to fade away if we look after the land, the water properly.

*Do you think if they build one LNG pipeline others will follow?*

Yes, it goes from a trail to a freeway. The people from Fort McKay, the elders there, said that they didn't realize when the tar sands started, that they had opened up a Pandora's Box. And they said, now look at it, it's just unstoppable. Fort McKay is a little reserve and it's completely surrounded by the tar sands now. So what was the answer going to be? "Oh, we'll move you." These are their homelands; this is where generation after generation after generation was raised. Now they can tell a story and you could see in their eyes. There's no life there. They can talk about when they were young, you can see the vibrancy in their eyes. You could hear it in their voice; you could feel the passion. And then they'll talk about today where they've got to fly in berries to feed us during our lunch. And their eyes go dead and there seems to be a lack of future there. Then, we asked, "Well, what do you think about your youth?" And then they start talking about suicide rates, alcohol and drug problems, because they don't see a future. The only future they can see is working in the tar sands. So, do I want that for our people? Absolutely not.

We're not here to hurt people. We're not here to starve people out. But we are here to make sure that people understand that, once something's gone, it's gone. You're never getting it back. That's all there is to it. They're not going to say, "We're going to borrow this from you and I'm going to give it back to you in ten or twenty years." Enbridge constantly says, "We've been in the pipeline building business for over fifty years." Okay, now tell us about the thousands upon thousands of oil spills. Anything man builds is going to break. Very first question we asked them, "Will you guarantee that there will never, ever be a pipeline break?" "No." That's the only honest answer we got back from them. At least we got one honest answer.

*Do you think it might be possible for the British Columbian government to push the Enbridge pipeline in order to weaken the opposition to the gas pipeline?*

Yes, I believe it's the old shell game. Look at this hand. Meanwhile, the other hand is doing something else. I love to put things in the most simplistic manner. It's like Homer Simpson: you'd be talking to him and he'll show you something shiny and he gets all distracted. They think we're all Homer Simpsons; give you something shiny.

*So that gas looks good compared to oil?*

Yes, it's like you're taking the lesser of two evils, but you still end up with pipelines and those pipelines can carry whatever they want.

*Once the gas runs out, they might end up shipping out the water to Asia.*

And we have some of the cleanest water. There are so many levels to this, and we do a lot of talking amongst ourselves and with our neighbours. What can we protect? What avenues do we have? What does the future look like? Who would think that you would pay more for water right now than you would for a gallon of gas? You go get a couple of little bottles of water and fill that same bottle up with gas and you're paying more for the water than you are for the fuel. And water is going to become a more and more wanted commodity in the future. You consider what, 2 percent of the earth is fresh water, and look at how much of it is here. So you know, they talked a few years ago about a trench between B.C. and California and that was strictly about fresh water.

There are many projects going on with oil, gas and coal, and it's the cumulative impacts that I don't think people are quite getting. This is a time that we need to stand up and say, "You know what, there's got to be one place on earth where you can keep and not just destroy everything and not have it come back." Forestry, we know up here that it takes seventy to a hundrerd years for trees to grow back to maturity, but do it so that it's spaced out. When the oil and gas is done, when our rivers are done, they're never coming back.

*You said that this part of B.C. is now on the world map. How have you been able to put it on the world map? What alliances you have been able to make with other groups?*

A lot of it has to do with doing outreach. Whenever I'd been asked to speak, I get permission from my fellow chiefs. Even though I am a chief of a clan, there's still four other clans. I get permission, this is what I want you to say and then they talk about what the response is. Number one: don't let the media control the Wet'suwet'en. The Wet'suwet'en have to control the media. A good example is I was at an Enbridge meeting and I was talking to Martin Louis. We were having a discussion and a hand came out of the side and automatically I put my hand out and there was the CEO of Enbridge and their thirty cameras went off. So now I know to look before I stick my hand out, because you automatically stick your hand out and I was the front page of the *Toronto Sun, Vancouver Sun*. I was right across Canada. A friend of mine from Germany sent me a picture.

But we have a website and we get questions from all over the world. "How is it going against these pipelines?" Especially when you get questions from South American countries, where they say, "Please don't let this happen to you, this has happened to us." The reality of the situation really hasn't hit enough Canadians. British Columbia is one of the very last provinces where we have what we have. It hasn't been damaged. I did my sixteenth birthday in Newfoundland and I loved it there. Then you got the offshore drilling happening. That's all it takes. I believe there are other greener options for British Columbia and Canada. Ten years ago I wouldn't have believed it, but with all the pressure we are getting from pipelines, from proposed mining sites, especially when they're going to use lakes for tailings ponds, it's becoming the norm. That's the problem. The biggest problem is it is becoming normal.

*There are just so many proposals going on right now.*

Well, for ourselves, we're absolutely inundated with proposals. But you can't say no to them all, but you sure can say no to the most dastardly of them. The prime minster of Canada said that First Nations people do not have veto power. Well, you know what? That still doesn't mean we can't say no. There's a difference.

Don't take it for granted what they tell you. Always ask questions and find out what do they truly mean. I don't believe we're getting the full truth. I don't know what the JRP panel will come up with, but definitely I see court actions coming. I don't ever endorse violence. I'll tell you why: because I was told what the true definition of a warrior was. They said the true definition of a warrior is that he carries the biggest burden of all and that burden is the burden of peace. Because he knows what the consequences of war are. So I'll never condone violence because it's my people that will suffer. If they want to meet us on the land, that's fine. We can make them stop. But would I condone violence? When the prime minster of your country refers to you as a terrorist, who's condoning violence? Who's instigating that violence? When we left British Columbia last year, when we went across the country, we left here as radicals. We got there and were called terrorists. Of course that only hit the papers once and then he pulled the wording out. There were 5,000 of us when we got there. And I asked Enbridge's investors, "Why did you guys put undercover RCMP officers and CSIS onboard a train with us?" They stick out like sore thumbs.

They denied it, and the following day, in the *Toronto Sun*, Enbridge admitted they did request that British Columbia, the RCMP and CSIS monitor us. So they did admit, within twenty-four hours, because we had to travel with lawyers, we had to travel with a certain amount of security with us, and every place we went, the crowds got bigger and bigger. But you know, the farther we went, the more support we got. But you're always going to get somebody that you never know, so we had to be careful. So when, I think it was the *Toronto Sun* again, asked me, how did I feel about having undercover RCMP and CSIS onboard with us, I said, "Well, I want to thank them." I said, "As a Canadian citizen, it's their job to ensure the safety of a Canadian citizen." Now if something would have happened to me, it would be their job to protect me. So I'm not going to fall into that media trap of pointing fingers back. So I just thanked them for the extra security that we had.

*What would constitute a victory for you? What is it that you're trying to gain ultimately?*

Well, you have to define what a victory is. I think if you want an overall, end-run game — a touchdown — I don't know if that is a true victory. You have to take victory in stages. I think that when it comes to pipelines in particular, you have to go at each and every angle that there is: through the courts, through the public, make sure their social licence is approved first. The elders always say that there are many trails to get to one point, but as long as you get to that point together and each avenue has been explored it's okay.

It's not the 1 percent that should be making the decision. And what I'm doing today and speaking to you, is part of that outreach.

*You say that there are many pathways that lead to an end point, but what's the end point?*

The end point is when industry is going to be responsible. And if we are talking strictly about pipelines, there definitely will be some that will be a no-go. There's got to be a better alternative. I don't mean the entire world going green, but why is all the pressure in British Columbia at this point in time? It's because they've exploited and used all the resources elsewhere. Do we really want to have people so concerned with oil and gas that they have to disregard everything else? That nothing else matters? The propaganda that's out there, they're making it seem it's a done deal. I hear that quite often, "What are you guys going to do after it's built?" Wait a minute; we're just having a discussion on it right now. You've already got it in your mind that it's already done. There are people overseas that are actually already thinking the pipelines are built. They thought, "Oh the way we were told, it's already done and they're already shipping." Well, in Vancouver they had some pipelines that they're shipping out; they don't have any in the north.

*But maybe that's a strategy to talk enough like this so that the opposition will go away in their mind because it's too late. It's already virtually there, so why oppose it?*

And that's it; it's just propaganda. The reality is they've got a long, long ways to go. As far as I'm concerned, we haven't even started the discussion. You know it's their mindset that keeps on bringing us back to the same thing: the monetary value. Well, what's the long-term profit? The profit should be in what's left, not what's gone. That's the profit. Simple, I love simplicity.

You see the signs around here, "Yes to jobs." That's an incomplete statement. There should be another one underneath it that says, "But at what cost?" There's a huge difference. We've got this mountain here, in our language Tse'Deh K'eh — Hudson Bay Mountain — they were going to take the top off it for molybdenum. It's ten billion dollars, it's a mountain! It's called Tse Deh K'eh. It's the woman that gives life to the valley. That's where the water comes from. But molybdenum, we need that, they say. I don't need that, I need a mountain, I say.

*You have used the term social licence a number of times, what exactly do you mean by it?*

The public has to agree.

*And you don't mean as represented by the government?*

No, I'm talking about the person next door, the person down the street and the people that are going to be extremely affected by these things, people that come here for that quality of life, to go out fishing in the river, to enjoy going swimming. Access to go out and look for wildlife, see wildlife, climb mountains. That's what we need to look at. People have moved here for a quality of life. Why would they want to risk that? How many people from other provinces, from other countries, come here for summer holidays? To enjoy what we take for granted, and we won't know what we have until it's gone. That's when you miss it. I've been to enough places where I can see what's going on, and I like what I have.

*The Smithers council has come out against Enbridge, hasn't it?*

Yes. We, the Wet'suwet'en, have a protocol agreement with the town of Smithers as well which gets renewed every year. The major part of that protocol is we know where we will not fully agree. So we agreed to disagree on certain things, but we have not said this is a game changer or this is the end of the game. Every year we discuss whether we are willing to go into another year, because we did talk about doing, possibly, a five-year one. But too many things come up in five years, we'd prefer to deal with them on a yearly basis and make sure that issues we have are put in front of them constantly. And they've offered us a seat on their council, and every time that they have a meeting we are fully aware of what's going on. We have a good relationship with Smithers, actually. I think it was at the Union of B.C. Municipalities, we went down there and we did a presentation in conjunction with the town of Smithers and simply reminded everyone that, if other communities possibly did this, they would have better relationships with each other. Especially when you have so many industries coming in. If you guys understand each other right away, everything is on the table; it makes it so much easier to move ahead. You know we're supposed to be friends and neighbours, so let's act like it.

*You seem to be quite a model for that, in Smithers, compared to some of the other communities where the divisions are more obvious.*

No relationship is perfect. But we've agreed in the protocol that we would agree to disagree. You know there are ongoing issues and that doesn't give us the upper hand. It doesn't give them the upper hand, but they still acknowledge the fact that this is Wet'suwet'en territory. And it was a municipality that was built on our territory and that's a good starting place. From there you can have the conversations. It's all about dialogue.

This Sunday we will be in Terrace, and it's just reminding Enbridge that no still means no. So I'll never forget what was said to us, they said, "Oh, we want to change your 'no' into a 'maybe' and your 'maybe' into a 'yes.'" And I just had to remind them — I think my grandson was five years old when they said that to me — and I said, "You know my grandson is five years old and he understand what 'no' means. He knows that 'no' does not mean 'maybe' and it certainly does not mean 'yes'. And you who are older than five years old and multimillionaires don't understand 'no.'" They were offended. And I really don't care if they are offended, no still means no. And they can't seem to get it. They're just so used to the almighty dollar being what it's going to take. Money does make the world go 'round, but they get to go home. Where do I get to go when it's all gone? I am home. I can't go elsewhere. My children can't go elsewhere. My people can't go elsewhere. They get to go home. We are home. And every decision we make affects everybody downriver.

From here through to the Skeena, down to the Haida Gwaii, right from here through the Fraser to Vancouver Island, that's all going to be affected by what we decide on pipelines. And then there's tankers. Okay, they won't sink, and they'll have double hulls. Well, what about the vibration of the motors on the sea life, you know? That affects the whales, the seals, the salmon, the herring, the crab. Anything that migrates, it still gets affected by what's happening above them, by these big ships. I was a skipper for twenty-five years so I understand that little bit.

*In terms of the pipeline opposition, is it just lots of different groups, or do you see some groups as being leaders of the opposition? First Nations, such as yourself, obviously have the legal case, which other, say, environmental organizations don't. How do you see the opposition working together? Are they all equals, or are there some leaders and some followers?*

I think we're working all together, and everybody has input into it. And then you discuss: "Okay this is what should happen." And you take the options that are out there and move forward. But, one of the things that was said was that we wanted to thank Enbridge for bringing us so tightly together, because we were all trying to do these things on our own. What happened is that we got together. We started having meetings and discussions about what we need to do to get to a particular point. And the more we discussed, the more people joined in, more First Nations and then NGOs and community members. They're starting to understand; it's all about education, education, education, discussion. And I believe that Enbridge did us a favour. For them to bring us together like that was amazing. It took that one huge project, and people started to realize the impacts that it would have. That brought us together, and once we had that, it made it so much better because we all had the same concerns.

*When did this happen?*

It wasn't that long ago, it was only about four years ago when it got really, really serious. That's when everyone from commercial fishermen, sports fishermen, farmers, loggers, First Nations, they all got together and said, "You know what? It is something that we all care about." When you start talking about water, that affects everybody. And it's that realization, and the realization that we can work together, and there are many, many issues that we butt heads on. We still continue on some, but when there's something that we have a common interest in and we know the importance of it, that's when we come together. With Enbridge, in particular, people just got tired of feeling that we didn't have a voice. So you get all the voices together and move forward.

*Do they come together through some kind of communication system? Or gatherings?*

We did a gathering of nations. We called it an energy summit, and that would be six, possibly seven, years ago. That's when we got people from Fort McMurray, Fort McKay, Queen Charlottes, the Haida, the Haisla and Tahltan, the Nisga'a, the Gitxsan and the Wet'suwet'en. And we just called it an energy summit and informed them: this is what's happening, right from the tar sands to the ocean, and this is what we need to discuss. We spread it out over three days, and we had hundreds of people attend. We also asked each one of them to bring water from their territory and food from their territory. Let's share some food and then we mixed the waters, and that's when we declared that the way the water mixes it doesn't keep it separated. It keeps it together, and that's how we need to move ahead. So we held the first energy summit, and they did another one, I believe, in Terrace, a couple of years later. We keep that networking going; as I said, last year I was up in Fort McKay and Fort McMurray. Then I'm always down in Kitimat or Prince Rupert or Vancouver. Whenever I have meetings down there, I make sure I do outreach there. It's just ongoing, seven days a week. I have a job here, but the overall job is being a chief and making sure there's something for our children. People are starting to realize that you don't have to sit back and just let things happen. You have a right to sit up and say, "I'm right here, I have issues, I have concerns." And use your voice. I believe that our people, and I'm talking about Canadians, we're getting lackadaisical about our political leadership. I think that we had so much trust in our past leadership that we really didn't monitor what's going on with Harper right now. And it's just, when you see what he's doing, people are starting to realize, "Hey, I don't agree with that." I made a statement in Winnipeg once. I really thought I was going to get in trouble for it, but I said, "You know in the past we've had some prime ministers that we were extremely proud of. You know we'll hold them in reverence." But with Harper, I don't think we will ever hold him in reverence for what he's doing.

*Your voice, is it a voice as a chief from your territories? Or is it a voice for northern B.C.? or a voice for B.C.? or a voice for Canadians?*

I think we're constantly being reminded in northern B.C. that we do speak for all Canadians. Because once people start to realize that things can be stopped, whether it be on a provincial, national or international level, it's just that realization that they can think, and "Hey we could have done that." We were told that British Columbia is actually a leader in Canada in how to deal with governments and industry and how to make them come to the table and have a true discussion. British Columbia is teaching Canada that the way forward is to say, "Come have a discussion. We'll discuss what's going on and let's take it from there. Just don't take it for granted that we don't exist." You know our existence is in every volume in this library, all this is the proof from the first round of the Delgamuukw case. I can't believe that right above my desk I have a saying, and it's from Gitxsan Chief Yagalahl, which says, "How can you say I don't exist? Can't you see me standing here in front of you? Can't you hear me talking? Why do you say I don't exist?" That was from the very first portion of the Delgamuukw case when they said that we didn't even exist. And that's what British Columbians, Canadians to have understand, that they do exist, they count, they matter.

# ~ Pat Moss ~

*Pat is a longtime conservation advocate and community activist living near Smithers,
B.C. Though best known for her successful sixteen-year campaign to stop the Kemano
Completion Project, Pat has also been involved in efforts to protect wild salmon from
fish farms, defend First Nations' rights and keep gas drilling out of the headwaters of the
Skeena River. In her career, she has played a leadership role in over ten environmental
organizations, including the Sierra Club of B.C., Canadian Environmental Network and
West Coast Environmental Law. For her role in protecting British Columbia's environment, she received the Governor General's Commemorative Medal (1993), Minister of
Environment Individual Award (1995) and Wild Earth Award (2002). Since 1996
Pat has been Executive Director of the Northwest Institute and for the last eight years
has also coordinated Friends of Wild Salmon, a coalition of First Nations, community
groups and fishing organizations in northern B.C. When not attending meetings or working on the computer, Pat likes to host Teddy Bear picnics for her young friends, take her
dog Pedro on country walks and watch foreign films.*

*We talked with Pat over a wild fish dinner in a pub in Smithers. The views expressed
here are personal and not necessarily those of either the Northwest Institute or Friends
of Wild Salmon.*

---

*Pat, you have been working on campaigns for over thirty-five years and so you've seen a
number of pipeline campaigns in your time.*

Yes, two major oil pipeline proposals and then a lot of other proposals for
different kinds of industrial development in the northwest.

*Given that you've got such a long history in this, can you tell us about what changes
you've seen over time in the campaigns over pipelines and the other development projects?*

The interesting thing from my perspective is that it actually hasn't changed
a whole lot. Certainly the way I work and the people I work with approach campaigns very much the same way, which is to try and look for broad-based coalitions
to work with instead of just searching out the likeminded. I guess the one thing
that's changed is there are more funded provincial groups with staff, and so that
has some impact, but as far as how we work in the north, that hasn't changed a lot.
In the late seventies the Kitimat Oil Coalition opposing the proposed supertanker
port at Kitimat was composed of a mix of unions, fishing groups, community and
environmental groups, as well as professional organizations. That was the first is-

sue I was involved in and everything else I've done since then we've used a similar approach. In order to have credibility in our communities, we have to include a wide range of groups, not just the "usual suspects."

Pretty much all the resource issues here end up relating to wild salmon. I worked for sixteen years on Kemano II, a hydroelectric project which was going to dam the headwaters of the Bulkley River and take more water from the Nechako and that's when I learned how deep-seated people's affinity for salmon was. Many proposed developments can be seen through the lens of threats to wild salmon and so that affects a broad cross section of people. I've always worked in broad-based coalitions and also closely with First Nations. That also goes back to my experience with the first round of the proposed supertanker port at Kitimat in the late seventies. There was an Oil Ports Inquiry established then, and our coalition was the major intervener for environmental interests and the major First Nation intervenor was the B.C. Union of Indian Chiefs representing First Nations. We had our own separate legal counsel but we coordinated strategy and met regularly. That's pretty much how I've worked ever since. Sometimes people talk as if they've just discovered First Nations can be allies, but in the northwest, First Nations and community groups have worked together in all the issues I've been involved in over the last thirty-five years.

*How is salmon so central to this?*

Well I guess it's everything. If you don't have the salmon anymore, you can't fish and you can't eat them. So any development that threatens the health of salmon stocks is going to affect people all along the watershed. I'm talking predominantly about the northwest but, of course, people in the Fraser watershed also care deeply about salmon. When I worked on the Kemano issue that was going to also affect the Nechako River, which is part of the Fraser system, people in Burns Lake, Vanderhoof and Prince George were concerned too about the impacts to salmon stocks. There were a lot of other issues but that was the most critical one, and that was what brought in the diverse interests, where commercial fishing organizations like the United Fishermen and Allied Workers Union and sports fishing organizations were involved. We even had the smelter union at Alcan as part of our coalition. A lot of those union members liked outdoor recreation and loved to go fishing, so they wanted to be part of our coalition too, which was highly unusual, since it was their company that was proposing the project.

*So their daytime interests were for the Kemano project, but their weekend interests were against it.*

They had some very enlightened people in the leadership of their union at that time, and it was clear that there weren't going to be many permanent jobs out of the project. There were going to be a bunch of construction jobs, but just like with many of the major proposed projects now, all the jobs are temporary in the construction phase and then you get very few long-term ones.

*When was Friends of Wild Salmon formed?*

Friends of Wild Salmon was formed in 2005, and it really came together around the concern about open net salmon fish farms moving into northern waters. Fish farms on the west coast have Atlantic salmon, and that's because they're more willing to live in crowded conditions. Our Pacific salmon haven't done very well in farms.

*And the Atlantic salmon do very well in these farms?*

They do, so it's Atlantic salmon that we have in B.C. fish farms. There has always been a lot of concerns about what happens with the ones that escape — do they end up breeding with the natural stocks. Also there are issues related to the farms themselves and the fact that, when you have that number of animals in close proximity, they need to use a lot of chemicals just to keep them alive. Because of their close proximity, they have a lot of disease like sea lice and because they are kept in open pens, the lice can spread to wild migrating salmon.

*So this would have been a major issue for your organization?*

Yes, it was a major issue. Everywhere in the world they've established open net salmon farms near wild salmon, there's been reduction in the numbers of wild salmon. Up until now, there haven't been any farms in the north, but we found out that the Department of Fisheries and Oceans had identified eighteen potential sites around the mouth of the Skeena, which is the second most significant salmon producing river in Canada. That alerted people to the fact that we could be dealing with a really major issue here and so that's how Friends of Wild Salmon started.

Again it was a coalition of First Nations, community groups, fishing organizations, both commercial and sports. Politically they were all across the spectrum and included organizations that don't see eye to eye on a lot of things. For example, there have been great debates between commercial, sport and First Nation fishing interests around allocations of different species, and to some extent there are whole different cultural mindsets around fishing. When it comes to big conservation issues though, there's a recognition that if we don't protect the resource, then we aren't going to have anything to fight about dividing. So going back to Kemano, I remember lots of times when there were people at the table who were also in the courts fighting one another or writing nasty letters about the other in the pages of the *Vancouver Sun*. However, on a conservation issue that threatened the very existence of the salmon, they were prepared to work together. So that's the type of coalition we have here.

Friends of Wild Salmon groups were also concerned about various other proposed developments like the first round of Enbridge's proposed pipeline/tanker project. However, as a coalition we decided we needed to maintain focus on fish farms. The individual groups were doing a variety of things, but as a coalition we really only had the energy and resources to deal with one thing at a time. If we started getting dispersed into a lot of things, we wouldn't be doing anything very effectively. We weren't involved in Enbridge at that time, and fish farms went on for three years until we were successful in getting a moratorium.

*How many farms are there now?*

There are none in the north. Lots in the south and the mid-coast area off Vancouver Island but we don't have any in the north.

*How did you get the ban in the north whereas they still have them in the south? How did the north manage to mobilize so effectively, or wasn't there the same campaign in the south?*

It's always easier to stop something before it's started than to roll back the clock and get things shut down. We were faced with the same thing on Kemano where we were saying "the Bulkley-Skeena is a pristine river system and there shouldn't be a dam here," whereas with the Nechako-Fraser we were dealing with a river system that was already impacted by a dam in the 1950s. As somebody said, "They want to take a paraplegic river and make it a quadriplegic." That doesn't seem as serious as taking a river that's in full health. With southern fish farms, I think most people realize it's not politically possible to shut down the whole industry, but they're trying to get the farms moved away from migration routes of wild salmon and they're also trying to get the farms into closed containment systems. We were able to get a moratorium in the north because the industry wasn't established here yet.

When we got the moratorium Friends of Wild Salmon had to have the big discussion of whether to disband having achieved our goal. Everybody basically said, "No, no. We spent all these years developing relationships throughout the watershed, we should continue to work together on issues threatening wild salmon." At that point the most immediate threat was coal bed methane drilling in the Sacred Headwaters.

*This was Shell's project?*

Yes. We had the Friends of Wild Salmon meeting in January 2009 and at that point Shell was scheduled to take rigs in there in June. We worked on that issue for about a year and then we got a moratorium, albeit temporary, there too. There were other people who had been working on the Sacred Headwaters issue already for a number of years and we worked in conjunction with them to get the moratorium.

At the very same time Enbridge resurrected its project and said it intended to go ahead with their proposal for a pipeline and supertanker port at Kitimat. That was when we started working on Enbridge and it's been our focus ever since. The first part of our campaign was getting support for a full public inquiry, and we did get a lot of support for that but the federal government had their own idea of how they were going to handle the review. At that point they were still thinking they were going to slide this project through quite easily, the way they had with so many other things. It became clear that the Joint Review Panel that the government had set up was going to go ahead, with or without us.

*Obviously the coalition stayed very strong and expanded with Enbridge being the focus.*

I work for an organization called the Northwest Institute and since 1996 we've been doing research and public education on resource use as well as convening different interests, especially First Nations and community groups, that often don't communicate with each other very much. Since Friends of Wild Salmon was formed in 2005 we have done the coordination for the coalition. In the case of Enbridge we took it a bit beyond our coalition as Friends of Wild Salmon has been based in the Skeena watershed with steering committee members from Smithers to Haida Gwaii. However, with Enbridge we've also worked with eastern communities, in particular Burns Lake, Fort St. James and Prince George. We have been linking with them, and that's been the northern Enbridge network, which is bigger than just the Friends of Wild Salmon groups.

*Linking up, does it rely on information sharing or joint campaigns?*

All of the above.

*What's the relationship between Friends of Wild Salmon and Northwest Institute?*

Well, Northwest Institute is a member group of Friends of Wild Salmon (FOWS) but we also do the coordination for the FOWS coalition.

*Who does Friends of Wild Salmon seek to influence? Is it local MLAs? Is it local public? Is it the provincial government? Is it federal government? Is it Enbridge? Is it the U.N.?*

It's not the U.N, but I'd say it's all the rest of those, but we haven't put a big focus on Enbridge because we know that there are other provincial groups that have focused on doing work with shareholders. Our focus is more on our elected governments — municipal, provincial and federal.

*Do you just focus on Enbridge, or is it also LNG?*

Everything I've talked about so far is in relation to Enbridge. LNG is going to be a much more complex issue. We've talked about sponsoring some public meetings just so people are more educated about, first of all what's even being proposed and, secondly, the potential downstream impacts. We also think it is important to understand more about the upstream concerns with fracking because decisions that are made on LNG projects here have a very direct effect on the northeast as that will mean increased development of fracking.

*How do you connect with groups outside of the watershed, not just east to Prince George but to groups in the lower mainland and beyond? I'm trying to get a sense of how those connections play out locally.*

Occasionally there have been tensions, and there's a history in the north of people being very resistant to outsiders making decisions about what should happen here, whether it's an environmental group or a corporation. With anything I have been involved in there has always been an initial stage of people getting to know each other and then a recognition by southern-based groups that there's actually a fair bit of sophistication and capacity in the north.

So in the first couple of years we had regular face-to-face meetings with groups from the north and south. We alternated the locations of meetings between Vancouver and the north and people began to get a better understanding of how the different groups were approaching the issue. Over time people just naturally carved off their own niches. Our forte was working within our local communities, and I think we were able to persuade southern-based groups that it was really counterproductive to have outside groups coming in or writing letters to local councils. For example, councils usually give a very different response to a letter from Greenpeace or Sierra Club than if they get a letter from a local community group. Generally politicians pay much more attention to their own constituents than they do to interests from outside.

There were a few little bumps in the first year or so but for some time now northern- and southern-based groups have worked quite well together. I think the network relies on having northern groups doing the work on the ground in their communities. If we look at where the presentations at the JRP hearings came from, there was a high proportion from the north. That made sense. A lot of people in the south signed up through automatic sign-up on the internet but I don't think people actually realized that they were committing to preparing a statement and going and presenting it. So, of the thousands that signed up in the south, only a small portion actually made presentations. Up north, again not everybody who signed up made a presentation, but a much higher proportion did because the project affects them in a very direct way. Not that you can't ever oppose something that isn't in your backyard but I think the whole campaign would be much more difficult if communities along Highway 16 were supportive of Northern Gateway. The fact that we're all saying the same thing makes the message much stronger.

*Looking back on your past thirty-five years, would you say that the capacity in the north for engaging in these campaigns has increased over time?*

Well, in the olden days, you had conference calls and we circulated our notes in the mail! Now, with the internet, there's a huge volume of networking, and that can be a problem all on its own. You can't possibly keep on top of it all because the Enbridge issue is linked into the whole tar sands campaign and we get lots of their messages too. I have a lot of concerns with the expansion of the tar sands, but my environmental work is really place-based. There are so few of us in the north doing this kind of work and there are many groups in Canada and the U.S. working on the tar sands.

*One difference, it seems to me and correct me if I'm wrong, is that over the last thirty years, First Nations have moved to the forefront in these campaigns? Partly as a result of the legal rulings, which have given them a firmer basis for their own actions. It seems that First Nations are playing a stronger role in opposition movements than they did previously, would that be true?*

Definitely. Remember when I said during the first round of the Oil Ports Inquiry in the late seventies, the Union of B.C. Indian Chiefs intervened representing First Nations' interests. Now you would never have that happen — you would never have all First Nations agree to have one organization represent them. At the Enbridge hearings, there are many First Nations intervenors and they don't all have identical positions. Also some First Nations chose not to participate in the hearing process and instead raise their concerns in other ways.

Certainly decisions in the courts have put First Nations in a stronger legal position. However, all the issues I've worked on since the first round of the proposed Kitimat supertanker port in the late seventies have involved working closely with First Nations. All the major initiatives, court actions, etc. undertaken opposing the Kemano project were done jointly with First Nations. Friends of Wild Salmon is a coalition of First Nations, community groups and fishing organizations, and this kind of joint approach has continued when working on fish farms, the Sacred Headwaters and now Enbridge.

*You have talked about the importance of local organizing. When Enbridge or the LNG companies or the federal government wades in, do they understand the local conditions?*

In the case of Enbridge, they didn't put enough attention into working with local people and getting local knowledge. Even Roger Harris, a former MLA from Terrace who worked for Northern Gateway, has spoken out since he resigned, saying that Enbridge ignored his advice. They seemed to have an attitude that they knew best. Enbridge is a big Calgary pipeline company and it is used to dealing with Alberta First Nations, who rely heavily on revenues from the oil and gas industry. However, here in B.C. they were coming into a very different situation with First Nations with outstanding claims who don't have treaties and who don't have a lot of industrial development on their territories for the most part, so it's very different.

*It makes you wonder if Enbridge and the federal government have some clever or strategic plan that they're working on, or if they are just blundering into trouble.*

I don't think they have a clever plan. Call me naïve but I think often the truth is not as complicated as people think. I think it is as simple as this big pipeline company (Enbridge) has their 'big oil' friends in power in Ottawa now, and they all want to see the Northern Gateway project go ahead. Even before the hearings started we were being told this project was in Canada's interest. They seemed to be saying that northerners should suck it up because the project is in Canada's interests, and it's only those foreign-funded radicals that are against it. Statements by the prime minister and Minister Oliver ultimately backfired though.

At the time, everybody felt under attack. That the prime minster and Cabinet would feel free to voice those views publicly made me think, "I don't know what's happening to my country." But the thing that I found reassuring was that even the right-wing media columnists weren't buying into this, and were saying "Oh come on, there's a lot of people that have concerns about this project and you can't just label everybody as environmentalists or foreign-funded radicals." There were even people that supported the pipeline saying that opponents have legitimate views and have a right to be involved in the process.

"Foreign-funded radicals" turned out to be a great galvanizing phrase in the hearings. Last year I went to all the northern community hearings. Initially I hadn't intended to go to all the hearings but everywhere I went people appreciated that I had come to witness their presentations. In a lot of places, there wasn't a huge audience because they held the hearings in the middle of the week, during working hours and sometimes in not very convenient places. The presentations were very powerful, and I wanted to see them shared more widely so the Northwest Institute produced excerpts from all the statements made at the community hearings. I took photos of presenters so we had pictures to go with the excerpts and we circulated summaries for each of the hearings from Haida Gwaii to Prince George. One thing that was really interesting to me was how many people started off their statements saying, "I am not a foreign-funded radical, but I am really concerned about …" and then there were the First Nation grandmothers saying, "What's radical about being concerned about your river and your fish?"

*So they appropriated the language, a big volleying point in response to Joe Oliver's letter?*

Yes, and we haven't heard Joe Oliver using that kind of language for a long time now.

*Were there any other big rallying points, that you saw during the JPR, such as the Kalamazoo spill?*

Yes, that was a case of one person's disaster is another's opportunity. While we felt badly for the people around the Kalamazoo, it was an important opportunity for us to highlight spill risks because it was the same company, Enbridge, responsible. There were similarities but there were also big differences because the spill occurred in a very populated area. If we have an oil spill in the mountains here, it's going to be a long way from population centres and difficult to access. Friends of Wild Salmon had the opportunity to highlight that, and we produced a brochure that we put in mail boxes all across the region. And then, of course, Kalamazoo has continued to be in the news over and over again, because it isn't all cleaned up as Enbridge was telling us. The last report from the U.S. Transportation Safety Board was very frank in talking about the company behaving like keystone cops. We used this for another pamphlet, which we called the 'Culture of Deviance', following the Safety Board wording.

*How has Enbridge responded in the face of this opposition?*

They're doing what all the corporate interests with northern projects they hope to have approved do. Alcan pioneered this approach in the eighties by supporting every conceivable worthy cause. Now if you have an arts performance you want to produce, a sports team that needs funds, a community event looking for a sponsor, you would be a good candidate for funding from Enbridge. And, of course, the airwaves and print media are saturated with advertising promoting Northern Gateway.

*Have there been linkages between the opposition to Enbridge and oppositions to Kinder Morgan and to Keystone?*

There has. When I was referring to the tar sands campaign, they're all linked through that. All the groups based in the south that have been working on Enbridge are also going to be involved in Kinder Morgan. There has been discussion about lessons to be learned from our experience. Certainly there are some, but in relation to the JRP, the whole environmental assessment process has been gutted by the government. We don't, at this point, know quite what the process is going to look like that Kinder Morgan will go through. It could be fundamentally different from our hearing process with the requirement that people have to fill in a ten-page form before they can even submit a written comment.

*They don't want a repeat of this Enbridge pipeline experience?*

Exactly, that's what I was going to say. We managed to generate so much interest and input that they don't want another one of these lengthy processes. When they come to communities that are going to be directly affected, I don't think that there should be a test. If you're a resident of that area and it's going to affect you directly, you should be able to speak. It's going to be interesting to see how they deal with Kinder Morgan since its terminal is in the Lower Mainland, so you could make a case that everyone in the Vancouver area is affected. The other thing that's different is that now the reviews of these projects have been delegated to the National Energy Board (NEB) and pipeline projects don't have any Canadian Environmental Assessment Agency (CEAA) oversight, whereas our process was a joint NEB/CEAA review.

In our process, the National Energy Board has been out in the region a lot. They had to deal with many questions and complaints about their process and they tried to make it more accessible. They know that they're going to have to do a lot more of that interface with the public in their new mandate, but the National Energy Board has had a very different culture from the Canadian Environmental Assessment Agency. They see things through a narrower lens. Now they will be expected to look at environmental and social impacts in depth whereas before while there might have been some of that language in their mandate, their focus really was on "does this make sense in terms of energy planning"?

*If we go back for a moment to the Enbridge project, what's the end of the process?*

Well, the final oral arguments happen in Terrace and then the panel has until December 31 to submit the report to the federal government. Then the federal government will make the decision. My guess is the report will be worded in such a way that the government will claim whatever decision they make is backed up by the report. That's how those reports are generally written; it's unlikely that it will say the project should not go ahead, but more likely will say that it can go ahead but under certain conditions.

*Would the government be able to allow Enbridge to go ahead without settling any possible, indeed probable, legal challenges from First Nations?*

I don't know. The case law says there is a requirement to consult and accommodate, but it's never spelled out that First Nations actually have the ability to say no and shut down a project. If you have a First Nation that's saying "no I don't want this happening on my territory," how do you accommodate around that? I think that it will probably take a few more legal cases to clarify.

*I'm thinking that for the non-Aboriginal opposition groups, having Aboriginal partners*

*is actually very important in terms of legitimacy, but maybe for the Aboriginal communi-*
*ties the reverse is not quite so true because they have alternative sources of legitimacy.*

I think there would be some people that see it that way for sure but I think
there's a general recognition that we need each other. If an issue starts breaking
down where it's seen as "the First Nations are just stopping development again"
and "this little community of 400 people is affecting thousands of others' jobs,"
there starts to be quite a racist undertone to a lot of the reaction. Whereas if it's
people who care about the future of our region, our rivers, our air, working on this
together, some of them are First Nations and some of them aren't, and that makes
for a stronger position for all of us.

*Yes, I remember the mine case in Williams Lake which ended up being split on Aboriginal*
*and non-Aboriginal lines and it was very contentious and often racist. How do you deal*
*with the industry view that what you're trying to do is stop development and stop progress?*

Well, one thing that we've always been able to talk about here in the Skeena
watershed is that we have a viable existing economy and a lot of that is based on
healthy salmon stocks. Is there any point in creating new jobs if we're putting an
equal or greater number at risk? That is undermining the existing economy because
so many of these jobs are only short term whereas the economy that's existed for
thousands of years based on the healthy fishery could go on in perpetuity if we
protect the resource. I'm not anti-development but it has to be development that
makes sense and is consistent with the values of the area and the economy that
exists here now.

*One of the issues that we're struggling with in our minds is that Enbridge has just been*
*such a poster child for what not to do and for everything you could possibly think would*
*be wrong in a project. Let's say Enbridge is defeated, is this just going to open the flood*
*gates for LNG?*

Yes, that's tricky, and as I've said before, it's a much more complex issue than
Enbridge because it's going to have to be more nuanced. It's so much easier to
just say "no we don't want this" rather than "these are the conditions" but we are
starting to have that discussion.

*And the First Nations have taken a number of positions with respect to LNG.*

The Wet'suwet'en have said they don't want any pipelines coming through their
territory. Some of the other First Nations have already signed agreements with LNG
companies. Other First Nations are interested in developing their own renewable
energy projects, and they see this as an economic opportunity to develop those
projects that ultimately could power communities, not just LNG plants.

*Does it play much of a role that the oil and the gas will go to China?*

Yes, it comes up but I think there is also the whole question of why are we exporting these resources at what, in the future, will be seen as fire sale prices, rather than using them for our own needs as we transition off oil and gas. We know that we have to start that transition but we're not going to be able to do it overnight and we should be using our fossil fuel resources to assist during that transition period rather than allowing massive increases in the development of the tar sands and fracking in order to sell off resources as quickly as we can to get the revenues now.

*Apart from LNG, do you see any other big issues on the horizon post-Enbridge?*

Well, there are lots of proposed mining developments. We talk about the gold rush of LNG proposals but in fact we are experiencing a gold rush generally in the northwest now with proposals for mines, pipelines, refineries, etc. I think there is this sense that we have a lot of development going on and nobody's stepping back and looking at it in a more comprehensive way. Each of these projects is on its own separate track of environmental review. We've been arguing that there should be what we call a "strategic environmental assessment" of all the various proposals to come up with some thresholds and guidelines that could be helpful to proponents also.

# ~ Nikki Skuce ~

*Nikki joined ForestEthics in 2009, the sole employee in the Smithers, B.C., office. Her current focus is in stopping the Enbridge tar sands pipelines and promoting green energy solutions. For several years Nikki worked with One Sky on policy and practical programs in Canada, Sierra Leone, Nigeria and Peru. She began to focus on energy issues after coordinating Canadian NGOs around the World Summit on Sustainable Development in 2002. Nikki has advocated for renewable solutions at the United Nations and at federal, provincial and local levels in Canada, and has hands-on experience installing solar systems. Nikki sits on several boards, including the Canadian Renewable Energy Alliance, the Wetzinkwa Community Forest and the Smithers Sustainable Advisory Committee. She holds a degree in Canadian studies and international relations from the University of British Columbia. Nikki's passion is creating social and environmental change at multiple levels. She lives with her Argentine partner, daughter Lucia and son Felix in a passive solar home they built on one of the local mountains. They enjoy skating on frozen lakes, heading out on canoe trips and hiking around (especially in search of morel mushrooms or huckleberries).*

*We met with Nikki, and her son Felix, in a small coffee shop in Smithers.*

---

*Nikki, could you tell us about ForestEthics and when you become involved?*

ForestEthics was formed during the Clayoquot Sound controversy. In realizing that the protests alone weren't going to cut it — which were exceeding all expectations (thousands of people blockading, maximum arrests, international media attention, etc.) — because the logging of old growth forests continued. First it was a coalition that formed which later became ForestEthics, which looked at market campaigns and who was buying the wood. It's always been a cross-border organization on the West Coast here in Canada and in the States. And while predominantly forest-based, it moved into energy issues, in particular because of the links with climate change and the need to address climate change and our dependence on fossil fuels, which is important for many things, including the health of the forests and the rest of the world. Frankly, you can't work on environmental issues without addressing climate change and energy issues.

I am the sole staff person here in Smithers, in the north. Merran Smith used to be up here as well. We worked on the coalbed methane issue with Shell in the Klappan, which was a huge victory in December 2012, although coal mining is rearing its ugly head with the new government. I started working on the Enbridge issue in 2009 given its threat to the region as well as to the climate.

*ForestEthics are based in California and Vancouver; how does that work coming into the north? Obviously you were working here before so you were known and are local, but there are so many other local groups, how do you coordinate working with them and not tread on their toes?*

A number of community-based groups formed in opposition to Enbridge. There is definitely and has always been a northern focus. Basically we had meetings early on with some northern and larger environmental organizations where northerners said, "Let us get the opposition, let us do the ground work that we have to do in the north because we can get the rednecks and the hippies, cowboys and Indians, the young and old folks across political boundaries to oppose projects that threaten, in particular, wild salmon. It's the biggest thing. And then we'll invite you guys (the larger enviros) in when we need you. Or, we'll use your resources to do things like a speaker tour and help raise awareness." And I think that worked really well. ForestEthics, because I'm based here, plays a more nuanced dance around that. It helps, just being here, knowing the northern tone and who the players are, being able to walk over to the Wet'suwet'en office and talk to people, knowing the media in the north and just not forgetting about it. In some ways it's partly the person who is here rather than the organization that people would think of in terms of working together.

*I see how you being a local person acts as a bridge. But what is the division of labour now between, say for instance, Friends of Wild Salmon and yourselves?*

We are able to work at the investor level, putting pressure there, such as supporting First Nations going to the Enbridge AGM, as well as using our strength in communications. Friends of Wild Salmon does an amazing job of coordinating communication between those community-based organizations and disseminating information and organizing regular meetings in the north. At times we're asked to help out, such as doing a media workshop for Douglas Channel Watch and that sort of thing. But, we also have an organizer in Vancouver, so very much work at building a large support base in the urban environments too, that are needed to oppose projects as massive as this. You need that, you need the resistance and the opposition along where the projects are going to impact. But then you also need it to be much bigger when it comes to something as massive as Big Oil. You just need everyone.

*We're still trying to understand how that all fits together, how you go from "I'm concerned about fly fishing" to "I'm concerned about the tar sands, concerned about climate change and concerned about capitalism." How do these different levels interact?*

I don't think everybody's there necessarily, making those connections with regards to the Enbridge pipeline. I'm sure you're aware that there are so many entry points to oppose it. There's the health of the watersheds and the salmon. There's First Nations rights and title. There's climate change and tar sands expansion. There's just this visceral response to oil tankers on the coast because of Exxon Valdez, for those around my age, those who remember. And they want to put oil tankers on the coast in the Great Bear Rainforest — this iconic area. Stopping tankers has rallied a lot of opposition. For some people it's the shipping of jobs overseas with the export of another raw resource and putting existing jobs at risk. There are so many entry points to opposition. What's been great is that it all allows for those broader conversations to happen. While you might agree to oppose Enbridge, you may be coming at it from diverse perspectives, but at least you can engage in a dialogue and have a conversation about climate change and tar sands expansion. Some people opposed to this proposed pipeline will support that pipeline to New Brunswick in terms of energy security. There are quite a few, I think, who oppose Northern Gateway because of these other reasons and not so much because of climate change and tar sands. We started off introducing it as such. We organized a tour called the Story with Two Ends and we had Andrew Nikiforuk talk about the ugly tar sands side of things and Ian McAllister talk about the beautiful coast side of things with storytelling and these stunning photos. That's when we were introducing this whole pipeline issue across the corridor and we've always made sure Northern Gateway was linked to the tar sands. Northerners have been afraid of using climate change as have environmental groups, people became a bit weary of having that lead the conversation. But it's there and, in particular, in the south, in Vancouver.

*What did you learn from being involved with the coalbed methane campaign?*

At the same time as coalbed methane was being proposed to be drilled in the Klappan (or Sacred Headwaters) it was also being proposed to be drilled here in Telkwa, which we succeeded in kicking out as well. And part of it first was this great woman Shannon McPhail. She was key. Organizations like ForestEthics and the Dogwood Initiative at the time had a ton of information about coalbed methane and the risks and the zero job creation aspect, the risks involved and what the impact on the landscape is. And there is the sad model of coalbed methane destruction in the northern States (Wyoming) where the land is scarred and people's taps can be lit on fire.

Anyway, we ended up organizing a forum with both sides on stage, which is what we often try to do here in the north. This is where we had such success in getting an open debate. We tried to do the same for Enbridge but Enbridge kept refusing. People want to have balance, they want to hear the balanced information.

So they don't want to go to the open house of the industry and government who just say everything is bells and whistles and shiny and you should say yes to it. And they don't necessarily just want to go to a speaker that we have that's going to show you all of the dirty, ugly things about it. They want to have both sides sitting on the same stage and sharing that information so they can make an informed decision and be able to ask questions, kind of like an all-candidates debate. So we had Shell and the Ministry of Energy, Mines and Petroleum Resources and the Oil and Gas Commission (which is useless). And I think too, that's what people found out. There's no environmental assessment associated with coalbed methane, nothing. And it's looked at on a per-well basis, not the overall 16,000 wells or whatever they want to have in there, it's looked at *per* well. And we also had Karen Campbell from the Pembina Institute and someone from Alberta who had experience with coal bed methane on their property. And I think we might have had Gerald Amos from the Haisla; we definitely had a First Nations representative. Maybe someone from the Tahltan.

This was held in Smithers and people came from everywhere. Karen was fantastic. Just that basis of informing people and seeing how inadequate the answers were on the industry and government regulatory side. Basically it challenged people's comfort levels and that really helped spur things and spur the solidarity, because the challenge with the Sacred Headwaters is that it's just so isolated. The bravery and power of the Tahltan elders and the women who stood on the line and got arrested blockading the road, much to the opposition of some of their own community members too, was incredible. That was the real flame in terms of starting the bigger campaign. As with Enbridge, we then mobilized to get municipalities to pass motions and people in the communities downstream giving presentations to their local councils.

And then you have enough of the ground support against the project, so that when the councillors and mayors talk to people, they're hearing the concerns, they're not hearing much support. Presentations to council are followed by a push to get the municipal councils to start passing motions against the project. That's what we did around the Sacred Headwaters and coalbed methane (CBM), as well as with the proposed CBM development in Telkwa. We've done that with Enbridge too. Then we start building on the communities opposed. The reason why we were able to get the moratorium against CBM drilling in the Sacred Headwaters is because the government couldn't find one single, not one single First Nations community, business, municipality or anyone who would champion Shell's project. Not one was supportive. The B.C. government had to do something. Had they been able to find somebody, they probably would have latched onto them and said "Well not everyone's opposed," just like Enbridge does — "Well we've signed on a couple of First Nations, so not everybody's opposed." Enbridge spins that all the time but they weren't able to do that with the Sacred Headwaters.

In addition to municipal and First Nations and general community opposition, we took a big ad out internationally when Shell's AGM was happening in The Hague. It was signed by something like fifteen international organizations and renowned people. And so that gave Shell a bit of a spook too. We continually had a presence at their annual general meetings and would follow them, would go to gas conferences where they were speaking and drop a banner or hand them an award, some direct action, and give out information and keep up the pressure. We found out where the president of Shell Canada liked to ski and tried to put up ads at the ski hill where she was. So constant pressure on the company from all sides while at the same there's all of that opposition up here and with the Tahltan.

Absolutely key was the First Nations in the territory outright opposed. We worked with the Tahltan, did workshops up there and helped disseminate information. At the same time, we were always working behind the scenes in terms of meeting with government. Always doing government relations, working with them, looking for solutions and continuing to keep the issue on their radar because once you get the moratorium, the pause button, it's so hard to keep up the pressure. The Tahltan, in particular, but others, like everybody else, we're being swamped by project proposals in this region. In Tahltan territory there are at least fourteen mega mines on the table, there's Enbridge, there are gas pipelines, there are energy projects, there's forestry — it's just overwhelming. So when you get the pause button, it's like "okay I don't have to look at that for a while." That's really the role that ForestEthics played. We kept the issue alive with the corporate pressure and the government relations, working with Shannon and her group at SWCC and working with the Tahltan and just trying to get a solution, not an extension of the moratorium but actually getting it banned permanently.

*Has Shell indicated that they want to come back?*

As far as we can tell Shell has only ever been kicked out or walked away from two other projects other than this one. One in Peru and the other in Ogoni territory in Nigeria. They have never given up. And that's it here! They probably would have held onto this tenure indefinitely if given the chance. But I also think that part of their motive is that they want to build an LNG plant in Kitimat and kept hearing from stakeholders about this unresolved problem up in the Sacred Headwaters that they needed to deal with. Shell couldn't start gaining social licence for LNG without solving their tenure in the Klappan. Cynically, that was probably their bigger motivator for walking away than all the rest of it.

*You mentioned the social licence and this keeps coming up, what does that specifically mean?*

You will always have some people opposing things but I think in terms of social license, it means working on a project together with the community, to make sure it's the right fit for the First Nations and the communities here and that there are potential benefits to it, that people could see and actually get. Versus, the empty promises.

*But how do you know when the social licence exists? For example, does Enbridge think they have it?*

No they don't think that; they know they don't have it for this project. I read *Oil Week*, a monthly industry magazine, and social licence is a big thing that companies are talking about now. Enbridge screwed up so much that they can never get it.

*So this social licence term, which is used in the NGO community, is this basically an NGO version of what corporations call corporate social responsibility? So companies say "We are socially responsible because we meet this CSR criteria," whereas you were saying "No, if you want to be socially responsible you have to have this thing called social license." Is this a correct interpretation of it?*

Industry uses the term social licence as well but it's interesting because companies like, for instance Enbridge, tick off a list all the time. They win corporate social responsibility awards (although I would not put them in the top 100 CSR companies). And if they are, that makes me think that the criteria is not strong by any stretch of the imagination. So they tick off their check boxes but then sometimes you see how they do it. For example, they call the office of the Haisla, the Haisla pick up the phone and answer, and Enbridge ticks that off as consultation. They called and somebody answered. Enbridge organized these community advisory board meetings and someone said "look I'm just coming in to observe, I want to see what these are about, I'm not being consulted" and Enbridge still ticks it off as having consulted. Who cares how many tick boxes you've hit when you do it that way?

People hear these stories and know. It might be good to define what social licence is. But generally it would need a loose list of criteria — there are some mines that would probably get social licence in this area. I might have concerns about them, but you weigh them against the need for some development and jobs, and if they are they not impacting wild salmon watersheds, if the company properly consulted First Nations and were up front with communities, and all these sorts of things, they'd likely get support. Not many projects make that criteria, that's for sure. There's a partnership with Patagonia, which was an investor for a salmon smoke plant. The fish, smoked fish out of Terrace, is a new enterprise that is working with

Babine Lake Nation catching up river. That would get social licence despite some potential opposition, such as from commercial fishers.

*With Shell you worked with the provincial government; the federal government was not involved. So is that the big difference between the campaign against coalbed methane versus Enbridge? You have the feds involved in the latter. What can you learn from the coalbed methane campaign and how does it translate over to Enbridge?*

I think we've applied a number of lessons in terms of Enbridge at a much broader scale. It's not like with some of our forestry campaigns where the solutions may end up with 70 percent conservation and thirty percent logging but with ecosystem-based management. This isn't negotiable like you can build one pipeline as far as Prince George and that's okay, or you can build up to twenty wells. These are "No's" so in a sense it's a bit hard negotiating. Across the board we put a lot of pressure on the provincial government to take positions on Enbridge even knowing that they don't have the veto, they don't have the final say, but that pushing a project through a province that doesn't want it is going to be really politically challenging for the federal government.

We have basically four pathways to victory against Enbridge. Firstly, Enbridge pulls out, which is the one we were focusing on prior to them submitting their application. We tried to inflict enough corporate damage so that they would withdraw the project, but they didn't. So now they're not pulling out and I think the ten secret $10 million shipper agreements was like play money for them to get through the review process.

The second path was getting a federally legislated tanker ban, which we almost got. We did so much work on getting all the opposition parties on board. This was another thing — the importance of working here in this riding and getting someone like NDP MP Nathan Cullen to champion the issue. We also did outreach work targeting Liberal MP Joyce Murray's riding for instance. She became the champion for a legislated tanker ban and helped get the federal Liberals on board. The Bloc Québécois was fairly easy to get on board given the issues linked to the tar sands and opposition generally to Harper. With Nathan Cullen's leadership, the NDP put forward a resolution saying that there should be a federally legislated tanker ban, which wasn't binding but it passed by the majority of the House. Joyce Murray and the NDP, I think Fin Donnelly, had private members' bills towards the federally legislated tanker ban. As they started moving those forward, we showed them the support on the ground and that votes would essentially go their way if they approved it. And then the day before Joyce Murray had a second or third reading for her bill, Harper called the election. The election of Harper's conservative majority government had him saying within twenty-four hours: "Well now we don't have to look at regressive energy transportation policies for the west coast," specifically targeting the tanker ban. So that was a blow to our second strategic focus. Thank goodness we didn't have just one strategy!

The third is within the process, and this is a hard one too, by getting the JRP to say no. The federal government changed the rules last year so, even if the panel recommends no, now Cabinet can overturn that decision; that wasn't the case before. I still think it's going to be politically challenging for them to overturn, if we can get the panel to say no. It's stacked against us, they've only ever said no to one project, but there's compelling evidence why they should say no, and in their interim report it came out with 199 conditions which would be needed for approval, which is pretty strong in terms of any other NEB hearing. Although Cabinet might say yes without all those conditions.

And then fourthly, it's through First Nations' legal cases. But always in all the strategies there has been B.C. public resistance and political resistance. If you have the support base, and you absolutely need public support in British Columbia, then hopefully it's a vote-determining issue.

*So in terms of the First Nations, how much coordination do you have with them?, Has it been possible to break down those Aboriginal — non-Aboriginal barriers?*

I actually think that this is the one aspect to thank Enbridge for — bringing together First Nations and non-First Nations communities. I know that's also been said by former Saikuz chief Jackie Thomas. There's still a lot of racism in the north. But opposition to Enbridge has really created a lot more solidarity, a lot more people working together, a lot more understanding. It's given the opportunity to break down some barriers, even in hearing stories and testimony, whether through the JRP or in rallies or just conversation. I think it's been huge actually, and that's the strength in the opposition movement, that it really has built bridges. I think the challenge is looking at how we keep these alliances to fight for what we want moving forward. How do we keep working together as closely as we have after we win against Enbridge?

*Would you say that the First Nations are in the forefront, the leaders, of the opposition of Enbridge?*

Yes, absolutely. One of the things that we helped bring about at the beginning, just co-facilitate, was called the All Nations Energy Summit in June of 2009 in Moricetown. Hosted by the Wet'suwet'en, it had First Nations from around the tar sands to Haida Gwaii and community members of all stripes. There was a lot of information sharing and at the end of it there was a sharing of the waters ceremony. It had an incredible impact to set the stage early on because companies play off different nations and try to divide and conquer. Which is what they still did, Enbridge had to increase the boundaries of those potentially impacted by the pipeline to gain support and try to squeeze the others out. But one of the things that the Summit helped do was dispel myths. For instance, one of the Treaty 8 representatives thought Enbridge was a "done deal." In the past they opposed a gas pipeline and got bulldozed over it (i.e., it happened anyway with no benefits to the nation). And so they didn't oppose Enbridge because they thought it would just happen anyway. They're just so disenfranchised, so impacted by development that to hear the solidary and the opposition say "over my dead body" and "There's zero way that this pipeline is going to be built" was like "Oh okay, we don't have to a sign a deal with the devil." The Summit was huge too in creating dialogue amongst First Nations who don't always talk to each other. Coastal First Nations are organized as a unit, but other than that there wasn't much dialogue. Now there are more conversations that are happening between and across communities.

Another thing is that ForestEthics has worked with Coastal First Nations for years, like for over ten years in terms of the Great Bear Rainforest. There was a recognition of the government-to-government relationship of First Nations and their rights and title. Conversely, it was recognized that "okay environment groups have some power in urban communities and can put political pressure and do markets pressure" and that there can be a meaningful role for ENGOs to play. We've maintained these relationships. There are times when we've screwed up. People screw up all the time. I'm sure I've made mistakes along the way. And we don't always agree on everything. But for the most part, there's a recognition of synergistic roles that can be played and the power that First Nations have. Ultimately that's one of the pathways to victory that is key — First Nations opposition and section 35. And yet recognizing capacity issues sometimes, being overwhelmed with all these LNG and other projects. So, for example, we ask if we can help with getting media out, or if there's interest in going to the AGM to talk directly to the board and shareholders and have it not be seen as consultation, or cooperating with outreach events or rallies. Other times, providing support is simply staying out of the way. First Nations are definitely strong leaders in the opposition to Enbridge Northern Gateway.

*How do you deal with the outsider-insider clash, which of course Joe Oliver tries to exploit?*

There's a lot of trust building that had to happen in terms of the Enbridge campaign. But, you know, the Enbridge supporters play on divisions and it becomes this meme of "oh you're American funded, large environmental organizations, you're being driven by outside interests" and that filters down. The sad thing for me is when it's repeated, I mean it was Oliver's meme and then it sticks. So you even have all these community-based groups that organized to oppose Enbridge and what they often said, when they started speaking soon after Oliver released his open letter, was "I am not a radical, I have not received any funding" and all these things. That's great, but it's reinforcing that so someone like me comes along and "yes, I am receiving funding" but hopefully for the better good. It was definitely a meme that stuck for a while and it definitely was a challenge. Because if you're a messenger and you're out in the media you want people to also recognize your authenticity.

*How would you look, just stepping back a little bit, at this whole resistance movement? Is it a question of the Indigenous groups fighting for survival and development getting together with the environmental groups? Is it the combination of these two movements or is it something else or more?*

I think it's even more actually because what I have seen is also strong union-based opposition. Whether it's from the tar sands, where foreign temporary workers are coming in because there's already maximum employment, or to the shipping out of jobs with no value-added happening here too. There are unions whose very livelihood depend on healthy coastal fishing, who have had jobs cut for so many other reasons. And those with just more of a social justice view, like the Teachers Federation, who are more in solidarity with First Nations than anything.

*So it's much more than environment, it's social justice. Does this merge with the anti-globalization movement?*

There's a challenge in that. I don't want to create any phobias; I don't want people to be anti-China, anti-Chinese, and there's definitely those sentiments that pop up but it's that message of how do you oppose without creating xenophobia. Here is more foreign ownership, here's less of our politicians being able to make the right decisions with FIPA and other things, and here's raw logs or raw bitumen just going overseas for cheaper labour overseas and we don't have any jobs. So it's more looking at it from, not just from a jobs perspective, but from resource control; we don't have a plan. What is our energy plan? Right now it's just develop as fast and quickly as possible at all costs. So how do you reign that in and come up with a strategy that maybe yes it includes LNG going over to China and maybe it doesn't. It's okay that we have these export markets but at what cost and what are we putting at risk? Enbridge is so easy on that front because there are not jobs and the few jobs that exist are not going to anyone who lives here.

But in terms of globalization, I think too the more you step back, you get these people saying "oh you're a hypocrite, you drive a car and you use gas so you should support this pipeline." It's like, wait a minute, now that doesn't correlate. We all need to reduce our fossil fuel use, but we also need political and corporate leadership to move us. And it's true, we do need to start having that solutions conversation: "What is it that we want to do?" That is, "How do we make the transition?" Again it's that leaping off point for these broader conversations that we need to have and we need to start transitioning to a post-carbon intensive future.

*So the opposition is questioning the need for a neoliberal form of globalization?*

What's interesting is that Shell was easy because of the fact, from Burns Lake-west, people have a huge distrust here, whether they're super pro-development or not. People have a huge distrust for companies that come from outside and tell you everything's rosy. So what's interesting with the Enbridge project is that they actually are Calgary-based. Shell is in a sense easy, they were foreign and they're an easy whipping boy, like who except perhaps Exxon is as bad as Shell globally? But Enbridge is also not from here and they don't get this cowboy, Indian culture that's up here that will unite. And so what's interesting is that there's also a cultural difference in Alberta and B.C. Roger Harris, who used to work for Enbridge, was told to "do it like they do it in Alberta" and was given a big fat chequebook. But he said, "You can't do that here in B.C., you can't do that, you can't act the same way," and they just said "Come on, just fill out what you need." It hugely backfired.

I think all these global pressures are recognized but people also live here for a quality of life and there's a heartiness to this northern living that people feel proud of. I loved hearing the story of that ship wreck that happened to three Haida fishermen who survived on an island for weeks last year. They were interviewed after saying, "We're Haida, of course we knew how to eat off the beach." There's this sort of resourcefulness thing. This resistance to these global pressures. We've also won some big fights (against Shell, against fish farms on the Skeena) and so I think that's huge. There's an empowerment here too — we know we can stand up together and win. Some of them are uglier and harder and we're not going to win them all, but we'll stand up and fight when we need to.

*You mentioned cultural differences between Alberta and B.C. It's a more capitalist culture in Alberta whereas here you obviously have a different kind of culture, both Indigenous culture but also a non-Indigenous culture that is concerned with a quality of life.*

On that, when the JRP first started and we were in Kitamaat Village, I took three Alberta reporters, Calgary-based reporters to dinner. First we went to Sammy Robinson's, who's a carver, a Haisla carver, and to which one of the reporters asked, "Would he be one considered unemployed?" I replied, "He's seventy and he makes like $300,000 dollars on a carving!" Not only was their understanding of First Nations different, but they revealed that Albertans mostly look through a lens of "How can we profit off this initiative?" Whereas British Columbians, in this area in particular, might first ask: "How will this impact our wild salmon watersheds and coast? What are the risks and what are the benefits to the region?"

Our town of Smithers, for instance, is diversified. We're not just a one industry resource-based town, similar to Burns Lake, so if your mills burn down, you're hooped. Here we've got resilience. When Gordon Campbell first got in and slashed public sector jobs, which is a huge employer here plus all the side contractor scientist jobs and the rest of it, there was resilience. People formed the Bulkley Valley Research Centre to continue doing a bit of science-based work. But we are a home base for mining, we do have a couple of mills. There's also fishing here, tourism. I mean former U.S vice-president Dick Cheney has a place here for crying out loud. It's huge, this is a steelhead and salmon capital, so it plays a part. But not just that, it's the quality of life as to why people want to live here, whether it's quietly sitting by the river versus paddling in it or fishing in it.

*To go back to where we started our interview, ForestEthics is a part of the U.S. foundation Tides. How have you had to adapt in the face of the federal government's rules on charitable status and political advocacy?*

We've always been a cross-border organization. It takes a little bit of time to get charitable status and that's part of why Tides organized to be able to do charitable work and ForestEthics Canada had always been a project under Tides. Tides was getting increasingly pressured because of the Enbridge work and because we have a tar sands markets campaign in the U.S. We convince Fortune 1000 companies to stop using tar sands fuel and hopefully open up policy changes. So we were high on the target list. The U.S stuff is U.S.-based, so they have their different rules about what they're allowed to do as a charity. We were always careful, we were guided by this 10 percent rule, which is you can do 10 percent political advocacy and we would always say where all the parties stood, follow the general rules that we're supposed to do. For example, here are all the positions on the federally legislated tanker ban. But Tides was getting increasingly pressured because of the work that we were doing, they were in a predicament.

*You were accused of working against the "national interest"?*

Yes, that's what they said. They called us "enemies of the state" behind closed doors. And then Joe Oliver came up with that open letter, which in some ways was the best thing that happened to this Enbridge campaign. People would say to me, "I vote Conservative but I like debate and so here I'm giving you a donation of 100 dollars in the name of the Conservative government." It was a huge spike in our opposition, but Tides was under increasing pressure. We thought that Tides does really good work and so the best thing we can do, and take a position of power instead of being bullied, is to get rid of our charitable status, break our relationship with Tides and become a non-profit B.C. registered organization, ForestEthics Advocacy. We can do a lot of political work and be more political and not worry and not keep ourselves to 10 percent, because with this particular government we need to do more.

It's been a bit liberating because of that. In terms of talking about what role we play within the coalition, we now often get asked to help with more political activities. Someone else might do a report and they'll say "can you release this" because they're worried about their charitable status. Government has succeeded in silencing some people; people are a little more careful. Federally, the Conservative government is taking this country in the wrong direction.

# ~ Shannon McPhail ~

*Shannon McPhail is a mother of two and lives in Hazelton, B.C., on the banks of the Skeena River. She grew up on a working ranch in the Kispiox Valley and has worked as a big-game hunting guide, a welder in the pipeline construction industry, a nutritionist, a national champion college and high school basketball coach and a whitewater rafting guide after her education in chemical technology. She sits on the board of the Victoria-based Dogwood Initiative and was recipient of the Community Enrichment Award for northern B.C. in 2013. She is the executive director of the Skeena Watershed Conservation Coalition, an organization she founded in 2004 that has twice achieved recognition as Canada's Top Ten most effective and innovative organizations.*

*We talked with Shannon in her kitchen as the Skeena sped by just outside the window.*

---

*Shannon, could you start by telling us about Skeena Watershed Conservation Coalition (SWCC), such as when it was formed and who are members of the coalition?*

SWCC became a registered non-profit society in 2004, and we are a group of citizens, several organizations and businesses. Our board members represent a broad cross-section of people in the region and they are:

Roy Henry Vickers — world renowned Aboriginal artist who lives on the banks of the Skeena River and is an Order of B.C. and Order of Canada recipient.

Gene Allen — local wilderness lodge owner/operator, retired logger and rodeo stock contractor

Lindsay Eberts — Vancouver/Seattle businessman, who recently retired and sold his international company Seattle Aero Inc.

Carrie Collingwood — guide outfitter on the Babine River (Skeena Watershed) and Spatsizi (Stikine Watershed)

Todd Stockner — fine woodworker and angling guide on the Kispiox and Skeena Rivers

Wade Davis — Vancouver-based anthropologist and National Geographic Explorer in Residence

Brad Wilson — Gitxsan business owner of the B.C. Historic Café in Hazelton

Skeena Watershed was born out of, well it's an interesting story, it was actually born out of pro-development, and I originally wanted to find my husband, who is a welder, a job and mostly welds on pipelines. But, he does lots of construction, and he still, to this day, works in the oil sands.

*He works in the oil sands?*

Yes, he is a welder in the oil sands, and he's gone a lot. He's gone 60 percent of the time, which is hard on us as a family. After thirteen years, we still really like each other and spending time together; he still makes me laugh and blush. This all got started when I tried to find him a job working for Shell in the Sacred Headwaters, drilling for oil or gas, which I knew nothing about. I come from a background that taught me environmentalists are a sort of tie-dye wearing, hippy, dreadlocked, tempeh eating, soy freak shows, right? They all smoke dope. They are all crazy. Well, my evolution has been a very steep learning curve. Pretty much straight up. My dad is a retired rodeo stock contractor, big game outfitter and was a logger for forty years. When you look up redneck, you will see the picture of my family.

So, I tried to get my husband a job, and in doing so I learned about coalbed methane. It's an unconventional source of natural gas that you cook your food on if you have a natural gas stove. Methane is essentially a pure form of natural gas. It's unconventional because of the way it's extracted using a method called "fracking." And, long story short, the more I learned about what it was, the more I started to question it. This was not a normal thing for me to do. I have always firmly believed that people who say we are going to kill the environment are basically "Chicken Littles." They run around telling the world the sky is falling. I believed that no government or industry could get away with those kinds of things here. I mean, this is Canada, right? This doesn't happen here. Essentially, that foundation of belief fell completely out from under me, and it was some of the hardest years of my life. The very foundation that I had built my life and my ignorant bliss on, crumbled away. I was always the person who was naysaying these hippies, and all of a sudden I'm realizing they are right about coalbed methane. So, if they are right about this, what else are they right about? It was a meeting with government that taught me about coalbed methane. I called them and said, "I'm hearing a lot of reasonable concerns. This coalbed methane stuff is going in the headwaters of our three major wild salmon-bearing watersheds. What the heck?" Government replied, "Well, how about a meeting to discuss your concerns?" And replied, "I'm sorry, I thought I called Victoria? That's a pretty big journey for a cup of coffee." She said, "Well, that's what we do. We consult with the public. We want people to know what's going on."

*So, you were just a citizen?*

I was just a citizen. The biggest thing I did back then was write the

Community Newsletter for Kispiox Valley, which went to fifty households. So, I was not exactly an important person. I was as average a citizen as one could get. Anyway, I went around and I talked to the community and I said, "Hey, government is coming up and they are going to talk to us about this." And at that point I was still trying to promote coalbed methane development. So, government was supposed to come up but refused when I called them excitedly and I said, "Great news, forty to fifty people are going to come hear you speak. You are going to nip this naysaying in the bud." I was so excited, genuinely excited. The woman from government cancelled her trip and said, "I will not come and meet with that many people. I will meet with you and one other person." I thought, well that doesn't make any sense. What a waste of money. You're flying all the way up from Victoria to meet with me and one other person? Then the red flags and the alarm bells started going off. I didn't know who to turn to, and my brother said, "Well there's this fella up the Suskwa, and he knows a lot about a lot and you should get him to come to this meeting." So, he did, and he asked what I thought where really simple questions.

Simple things like — "That's pretty big, you are going to drill a lot of wells, thousands of wells. Hmm, has it ever been done where there is salmon?" Answer "No." "Has it ever been done where there's fish?" "Yes." "And how has it impacted fish?" "Well, negatively. It killed the fish, but we have new technology." "Okay, well, has it ever been tested?" "We are going to prove how good it works." "With our wild salmon in the Stikine, Skeena and Nass Watersheds, are you kidding me? Okay, well when does the environmental assessment come in? I'm looking at your process timeline here and I don't see an environmental assessment." "Well, there isn't an environmental assessment." "No environmental assessment? You want to drill thousands of wells in the headwaters of these three watersheds, three important wild salmon watersheds and there's no assessment?! And, you are not going to supply local people with jobs because it's a specialized form of drilling. So, we don't get jobs. We don't get the benefits out of this but we have to take all the risks?"

*What year was this?*

It was 2004. "You've never tested this and there's no environmental assessment?" And then, it hit me, these guys aren't interested in looking out for us northerners at all. Whoa. As a result of that meeting, it was government who essentially converted me into becoming a conservationist. That's the point where my whole world just crumbled. We have always had salmon in that river. I grew up fishing with my whole family, my grandparents, cousins, aunts, uncles, etc. We are all connected to this river. Every single person who lives here has salmon in their freezer and in their pantry. I'm getting down to the bare bones now because it's spring, but I still have at least sixty quarts of salmon. It will keep me until I'm canning in July and August again. They were putting our wild salmon at risk, I couldn't believe it. Wild salmon are a $110 million a year industry, just in the Skeena watershed. Guide outfitting, just in the upper Skeena, is $28 million. So, every seven years we are making a billion dollars from keeping our system intact. And that doesn't include the guide outfitters in Tahltan country, 80 percent of the guide outfitters up there are Tahltan. So, we are talking about a major economic impact. We are trading one industry for another. We are trading our local industry so a company with a head office on the other side of the planet can profit.

*Did you have a conversation with this government person on this?*

We had countless conversations. It was the economic argument, I think, in the end, that resonated, it was common sense. Some people call it environmentalism, but I call it 'common sensism'. The people who live here get it because we endure the long winters together, we are still connected to the river and as a result, we are connected to each other. Last night, we went to this focus group for a York University student, who is studying reconciliation for Aboriginal people in Canada. There were lots of different people there, and a woman who has lived here for a few years from Toronto who had never met a First Nations person until she moved here. She thought she was a very culturally diverse person, I guess because in Toronto you've got Little Italy, and there's the Koreans over here and this whole centre is people from India. Her school was comprised of students from all different cultures and she said, "I just didn't really see racism. Then I came here and I met the first people of Canada and I didn't actually realize that we still had First Nations in Canada. I thought all the First Nations were from the U.S., didn't learn about our own First Nations in school." I thought, that's interesting, this woman is well educated and grew up on one of Canada's major cities and this was what she knew of First Nations.

Anyway, people here depend on our watershed. Our livelihoods and our economy is dependent on the health of our watershed because so much of our economy and our sustenance comes from it, and it's hard for outside people to relate because they don't understand that connection. But, if you are First Nations, you have one traditional territory. You don't get a second chance. And in my family, which has six generations here, moving for me is not an option, even if it's the norm for the rest of society. If you don't like the pool or you don't like the hockey team or your teacher or the shopping, then you move. It blows my mind. Up here, in the north, if you don't like an aspect of your community, it's up to us to make the community better, to make it what we want, because moving isn't an option. This is where my roots are. This is where my family is. And the First Nations, this is their traditional territory, and they don't get another territory or another chance. If it gets destroyed, there's nowhere else to go.

*The decision-makers in Ottawa don't have the mindset that understands this.*

I agree. But we have been labelled as environmental radicals. Well, let's talk about radicalism. Digging the world's largest open pit mine for oil, sucking something out of the ground, using natural gas to separate it, gas that we also had to suck out of the ground, pumping it through these giant pipes that have the very potential to destroy what we need to survive. And saying that it's in the best interest for Canadians, that's radical. Drilling 10,000 wells in the Sacred Headwaters to pump out this gas, I mean, to me, that's radical. Anyway, so that's how Skeena Watershed Conservation Coalition came into being.

*So, the government person came up, met with you and the other person.*

Yes, met with me and one other person, and then I went around and I told my community what I had learned. My community, my peer group, my circle of people are the hunters. They are rod and gun club members. The old rednecks, the people who likely voted Conservative. I mean, that's who I voted for. I voted for Harper back in the day. And, because that was my circle, that was my community. I just knew that all I had to do was go out and tell people what was going on, and people would just stop it. I was so naïve, I didn't know.

Anyway, the Skeena Watershed Conservation Coalition was formed by loggers and ranchers and miners and drillers and welders and farmers, and First Nations, because that's what our community is. When people talk about our region, the USA have their version of cowboys and Indians, but a little differently up here, we are all on the same side. Our Kispiox Valley Rodeo, which was last weekend, had at least 50 percent if not 60 percent of the competitors from the First Nations of B.C. and Alberta, and the very first rodeo was on the Kispiox Village Reserve. So, when I say, we play cowboys and Indians, we really do play on the same side. We, the white folks, are the minority here. I'm non-Native, 85 percent of the population here is Gitxsan. And so, as a minority, you absorb the culture of the majority. Hence, the connection to river, and the culture and the history, and the knowledge that this is my home, this is where my roots are. It's the only place. It's where I want my kids and my grandkids to grow. And so, damn right, we are going to fight for it. And some will call us NIMBYs for doing it, well if you can't protect your own backyard, then what are you going to protect? SWCC was born out of that mentality. No one else is going to stand up for our home and our community.

*So, then where did it go? After you got formed, how did you take on Shell and beat them?*

Well, we didn't take on Shell alone. My family has some history with the

Tahltan. My Dad used to horse trade with one of the old Tahltan guide outfitters, Fletcher Day. He used to take his big prized stallion, named Simon, after Simon Gunnanoot, who was a famous Indian outlaw from here, known to have eluded capture for thirteen years, longest manhunt in Canadian history. So I went up and spoke with some of the elders, like Loveman Nole, who knew my grandparents, Marty and Dorothy Allen. My grandparents used to pick huckleberries in the fall in the Barrage burn on Tahltan territory, north of here where there was a forest fire. Forest fires propagate berry growth. They would spend a week there picking huckleberries together and they would come back with a thousand pound of huckleberries. Because of that shared history, I was able to get involved and other organizations got involved also, some before us and some after us. We held the first ever public forum on coalbed methane, didn't know what the hell we were doing. Didn't know that it was something that would likely be impossible to make a reality, so we just asked for it and got it. There were all these environmentalists who came to the forum and asked, "Who are these people? How did they get the Ministry of Energy and Mines and the Oil and Gas Commission and Shell to be on a panel for a public forum?" They came out to the event, and they were checking us out, asking who are these rednecks and we were sort of checking them out, asking who are these hippies? But looking back, now that I know them, they're not actually hippies at all.

*So, where was that held?*

In Smithers. On the panel we had Will Horter from the Dogwood Initiative and Casey Brennan from Wildsight to give some perspective to the audience in contrast with government and Shell. There was also Bruce Hill from Headwaters Initiative, who had been working with the Tahltan for quite a while. Merran Smith, then of ForestEthics and who now works for Tides Canada. At first, I didn't realize what a plethora of knowledge they had. I mean, I was just this young, feisty cowgirl. We organized a rally in Smithers, in really, really conservative Smithers. And, six hundred people showed up at this rally in downtown Smithers.

*What do you think brought them out?*

I had gone on tour, talking to everybody I could, chambers of commerce, rod and gun clubs, community associations, mayors and councils, regional districts, band councils, treaty societies, and I basically built a presentation about what is coalbed methane, how it works and why are we worried. We had done this tour ahead of time, and we didn't plan on doing a rally. We just wanted people to know what was going on, and we said, "We don't think you should just listen to us. Because we've talked with Shell and we've talked with government and we think you should invite them here and listen to them, and then you should make a decision about whether or not you think this development is a good idea." So, they did. They invited Shell to make presentations in various communities and 100 percent of those communities then voted in opposition. They heard from both sides. We didn't ask people to make a decision just hearing from us. We knew it was important that they got both sides. And that was why we had the public forum and people came to the public forum.

People came from all over the north. The Tahltan came down, six to nine hours of driving from their various communities, and people from the local community came. We booked a small hall that held two hundred people, which we thought would be way too big, and there were people lined up outside. I had just made moose meat chili to serve as food with homemade buns. People made comments like, "Moose meat? We are vegetarians." And I was like, oh, vegetarians, that's what food eats. Anyway, we ended up hosting this rally. Six hundred people come out. It was on Wet'suwet'en territory, so the Wet'suwet'en opened it. And then the rally march was led by the Tahltan youth who carried a big banner. We did our speeches in the back of a one-ton pickup truck. We put a microphone in and I got really pumped up because there were so many people there. I was like, "Do you know what I want to tell Shell? This is what I want to tell Shell." And I flipped the bird.

That's when Merran Smith was like, "Okay, we have got to tone this cowgirl down and we have got to direct all this energy that she clearly has, because she's obviously not going anywhere. Nobody's paying her, she and some other local yocals cobbled together this organization, They are paying for all their work out of our own pockets to do this." So, Merran told me that I needed to go to the Canadian Environmental Leadership Program, which is on Cortes Island. It's run by the Hollyhock Institute, it's five days and she would find the money to send me. And I was like, "What is that?" "Well, it's where you learn to be a leader, and you know, you learn about personal ecology." I was like, "It sounds really hippy to me. I am not going." So then she said, "Well, let me get you some information." The first thing I see on the agenda is you can meditate and do yoga in the morning, and I'm like, "No way am I going. Meditation and yoga? Forget it." And she said, "Look, I have somebody who will give you $5,000 for your campaign if you go."

We were paying for everything out of our own pockets. Rallies, public forums, posters, info sheets, all of that stuff. So, I went. In the first two hours I was there, I was furious because I didn't know before I got there that it was vegan. "You've got to be kidding me." The first thing on the agenda after breakfast was singing for social change. So, we spent an hour every morning singing songs from the social movement and the civil rights movement and the environmental movement. So, I was livid. I just wanted to go home. You have to take a jet boat ferry to get there. It's not like you can just drive home. I was four months pregnant and I just couldn't handle it. There was even naked hot-tubbing.

*It was your worst nightmare coming true.*

It was my worst nightmare, totally. But, after day one, it was the beginning of a major life change. It taught me how government works because at that point I thought MP meant military police and a cabinet minister was a really good carpenter. I learned the history of the environmental movement, and I learned and met people who were doing things and realized, wow, people are dealing with this kind of stuff all over. And there are other people who started similar to me, and I learned a new appreciation for these people that I had spent almost my entire life mocking and thinking they were wing nuts, and realizing, wow, they are actually really smart. And they understand it. I came home with a whole new way of thinking. All of it was thanks to Merran Smith and her foresight to just sit me down and look me straight in the eye and say, "You need to figure this out. You cannot work with government and collaborate on solutions if you are a street fighter."

Merran was an asset that we had, and she ended up being one of our greatest strategic advisors and helped us really figure this out, and brought other people in. So then we did what we do best, and that's gab. We went out to the communities and just spread the message, and asked people to hear Shell's message and then make a decision. And the decision that they made was to oppose it. And that's where our power comes from, our community. The only thing that we are advocating for is that the people who live here should be the decision-makers. And that's a really powerful place to come from. So, we always try to do things that are community building. Campaigning, it has to be community building. But, in all of this, we get a ton of the credit, but we don't actually deserve it. We have worked our asses off, absolutely, but it started with the Tahltan elders and it ended with the Tahltan. They are the ones who negotiated the solution. They and government, actually, negotiated the solution with Shell. We didn't. We applied pressure and created the conditions to make it possible, but they were the architects.

*The solution was the moratorium?*

In part, the moratorium was brought in in 2008 until they could figure something out more permanently. At the end of four years what they figured out was a permanent ban on all oil and gas activities in the Sacred Headwaters, and Shell voluntarily withdrew their tenure and then permanent protection against oil and gas was put in place. But, it didn't protect against the massive coal mine that wants to remove most of Mt. Klappan, which is right in the heart of the Sacred Headwaters. Now we focus hard on the Sacred Headwaters, because that's where we cut our teeth.

*Do you see yourselves as being part of a larger movement?*

There is the bigger movement, which is about climate change. And climate change, to me, it didn't resonate at all. Until this year actually. And, regardless of whether you think humans are causing rapid climate change or whether you think it's just a natural cycle, nobody disagrees that it's happening. And, because we are so busy fighting about what is causing it, nobody is really planning for adaptation. I saw the climate change maps for this river, the Skeena River, which is cited as one of the top hundred most resilient rivers to climate change, which makes you feel really good. But you don't realize that in my lifetime, by 2050, there will not be enough salmon in this river that we will be able to fish for them, if there is any. And that's a reality. It's not fear-based, it's science. Less than 50 percent of the tributaries of this river will flow year-round, and the sockeye don't really spawn in the main stem. They are lake spawners, and the sockeye are our main food fishery. So, without those tributaries running year-round, we don't have salmon. And if we don't have salmon, I mean they are a keystone species, we don't have much of anything. If you pick a leaf off of any of these trees, or a needle out of any coniferous tree in the forest, you find salmon in the form of nitrogen. They are the base of our ecosystem. Climate change is real, it's happening, and we are going to bear the consequences of it. So, we are doing some work to get folks educated about that, but the more local movement isn't actually environmentalism. We don't differentiate between a community, environment and economy. It's a three-legged stool and you can't plan for one without planning for the others.

*So you are talking about the defence of people's livelihoods and communities?*

Yes, too many people want to make a killing and they don't want to just make a living. Yvon Chouinard [founder of the company, Patagonia], who has, since I started doing this, become a friend. He made one of the most interesting statements I've ever heard, and he said, "You know, there are only forty businesses that we have found in the world that are over 200 years old." And he said, "They all have one thing in common, they don't grow." To make a long story short, he was saying this view that communities and businesses have to grow every year, that they have to increase is bullshit. He said, "It's a pipe dream. It doesn't work. Because, at some point, you've got to reach your optimal operation. If you keep growing, then you become a big machine and you just consume." He told me and the others around the dinner table that night there was one business that he found in Greece that is seven hundred years old, and they have been the same size. They have the same number of employees and they are in the business of plums. And they don't get any bigger. And he said, "We did a feasibility study, what would Patagonia be like if we didn't grow? If our development plan was not to grow at all, zero percent growth." He said, "You know what? We would still be profitable."

*The problem is that the capitalist economic system requires growth, is predicated on growth. So, you're really talking against capitalism.*

Yes. Well, there was a statement made in the Village of Telkwa and one of the counsellors for the village made a statement in a council meeting. He said, "They're talking about how are they going to increase growth? What new buildings are they going to build?" And he said, "You know, we get giant pot holes in roads and we've got some municipal buildings that are falling in, and we have a park that really needs repair." He said, "Instead of putting our money towards growth, why don't we put our money towards making what we have better?"

*I'm just wondering people like us, academics, like to put labels on things. How would you describe the larger movement? Is it much more than an environmental movement?*

Much more. I mean, all the people who are fighting against the Enbridge Pipeline, the minority of them are environmentalists. The majority are just common-sense people. Farmers, for example, who realize that if you overplant your field, your crops are going to be stunted.

My husband, who works in the oil sands, the majority of his work is welding on pipelines there, I mean we would benefit more directly than anybody else who lives here. He would have the opportunity to work closer to home. He's got two welding trucks. He could contract them out and we would make a mint, no doubt. But, he was one of the first to oppose this pipeline, and so were all of his co-workers. They have 'No Pipeline' stickers on their trucks in the oil sands, and the reason is that they look at the Enbridge pipeline the same way people look at raw log shipments. You are shipping our jobs to China. We should be building refineries in Canada, refining it here, and that's his opinion. And we would have long-term jobs, instead of just welding a pipeline to export our jobs somewhere else.

We've seen boom and bust here. It's something that we are all too familiar with, with logging, and we've had a gold rush, we've had mining booms before, and the story never changes. People come in, they make promises and then they claim bankruptcy, they don't pay their bills, and it is still happening. But what we are seeing happen now is companies are getting smarter. They are learning from Enbridge and they are learning from Shell and they have all these pipeline companies coming in now for natural gas, which I think is actually even a worse situation than Enbridge.

*In what way?*

Not in the environmental way, but in the economics way. I'm not talking about fracking, because that won't happen in our watershed until they finish fracking the hell out of northeastern B.C., but they need huge amounts of power to liquefy the natural gas to export it. Site C Dam is proposed to produce 900 megawatts of power. The medium sized terminal that is being proposed in Kitimat for LNG will need 800 megawatts of power, and there are twelve terminals proposed, twelve pipelines are being proposed. We are told that there is a hundred-year supply of gas, but a hundred-year supply at what rate? Nobody will tell us what that rate is. So, there is a hundred-year supply with one pipeline, or one terminal, but we have twelve proposed.

Are they going to build all this infrastructure for ten years of export? Our office has never been so inundated. None of us got into this because we wanted to be career conservationists. None of us. But, that's what we have been forced to become.

*But you know, the beauty of these pipelines is that even if it runs out in ten years, well then they can be used to ship something else.*

Put a natural gas pipeline in and convert it to oil, the only thing you have to do is trade out the pumping stations. That's it. You just need a different kind of pump. While TransCanada Pipeline company was in our communities telling us they would never convert their proposed gas pipelines to oil, they were in the process of trying to convert 3000 kilometres of their gas pipelines to get oilsands bitumen out east.

*Obviously it's been quite easy to go and oppose Enbridge for any number of reasons. But, is opposition now growing to LNG?*

LNG got out ahead of us, actually. So, it is difficult. And so, people say, "Well, it's not oil. It's just gas. If that pipeline breaks, it just goes into the air." And so, we don't realize the cumulative effects of what that means. Once you have a pipeline corridor, you have a pipeline corridor. And it can become oil or water or what have you. Once you have a pipeline, you can have multiple pipelines in that corridor. You have powerlines, compressor stations, fracking, emissions from the terminals, tankers, etc. You can put in all this infrastructure. We don't have oil and gas here, we have never had oil and gas here, and we want to keep it that way, and we have people who have moved here as oil and gas refugees. That's how they identify themselves.

What we need is community economic development, or economic development that helps bring people out of the margins. Development that makes them thriving, resilient community members. Because right now, people who are pushed to the margins, when you look at it strictly from an economic perspective, they are a burden to the taxpayer. So, there was this great study in Calgary, where they followed homeless people for a year, and they discovered that it costs more to the taxpayer to ignore them and leave them on the street than it did to build appropriate housing. If you don't deal with these issues, the rates of FAS (fetal alcohol syndrome) are going to continue to increase, and so is the unemployment. So, we have to deal with these issues. There is an organization here in town called Storytellers Foundation, who is doing an incredible job in leading this style of work. They are taking youth who have all of these hard issues going on in their lives and giving them work skills in a nurturing and caring environment. So, those are the people who are working at the Skeena Bakery. And the Skeena Bakery model is not to make money so that they can profit. Their model is to make money so they can hire more people. That's their business model. And it's working!

*Yes, again, non-capitalists forms of development.*

Yes. Storytellers is working with youth and women. They work with the Senden Agriculture Demonstration Centre. Local youth plant that entire giant garden and greenhouse. They harvest it. They tend it. They take the food. They preserve it. They sell it. They make salsa out of the onions, tomatoes and peppers, and cilantro. They do all these value-added things and sell them, and the community buys them all. That's how they make their money to keep going. You've got these gangster-style looking Gitxsan youth going to the Bulkley Valley Fall Fair in Smithers, and they are putting their vegetables that they have grown and their preserves into the competition, and there's these little old ladies sitting there looking a bit terrified of these gangster guys, who are actually sweethearts. My favourite is a guy with his hat on sideways, he's got chains around his neck and he looks like a little thug. But, he's around this giant zucchini and he's doing the rock symbol. "Yeah, this is my zucchini, it's got a blue ribbon. See that? It's a blue ribbon. That's my blue ribbon!" And they are so proud. Storytellers Foundation is doing all this stuff, they even have a youth catering business and it's the youth who do all the catering.

*That's a really fantastic story.*

Yes. They are doing all this in a way that's culturally appropriate. They work with the Gitxsan, they design these programs with the Gitxsan. They recognize that 85 percent of our population is Gitxsan, so we need to have Gitxsan teachers at the schools, etc. Our students need to be learning Gitxsan. The building across the street is the Language Nest, it's for kids zero to four, and it's a 100 percent Gitxsan. There's no English spoken there. And, my son, who is not Gitxsan, goes to school at John Field Elementary and is in the French Immersion Program, but he spends two days a week, forty-five minutes each time, learning Gitxsan. And now he speaks more Gitxsan than I do. And it's such an amazing place to be that we get the opportunity to do that as non-Gitxsan people. Looking at Hazelton as a whole, this house is municipal, but that over there is reserve. And the building there is municipal, but the building beside it is reserve. So, we are an integrated community, and it doesn't mean it's always easy, but it works because our cultures co-exist and we can learn from each other.

*It's a good alternative to mega projects as development. This is what development should look like. So, you are trying to hold on to a non-mega project, non-growth oriented community?*

Well, it's not that we disagree with mega-projects. We supported Galore Creek, when they wanted to build their massive gold mine, it was going to have huge environmental impacts. No doubt. But we supported them heart and soul because they bent over backwards to gain social licence. Projects don't proceed here without social licence.

*What do you mean by that, social licence?*

Social licence means that you have the blessing of the community. Nathan Cullen, our MP, built an entire report on how to earn social licence and what things we need as northern communities to support projects. Nathan went to all the communities to figure out the criteria by which we could say yes.

*That's a good description then, blessing of community?*

Blessing, yes. It's much more involved than that and very different from the traditional method of operation where you come in, you consult with the community, which means you host an open house and you dictate what you are going to do, and then you write down people's concerns, which you promptly ignore and you proceed anyway. We have seen that a bazillion times. But, Galore Creek had meeting after meeting with communities, and they listened. They said, "We hear your concerns. What are the solutions? We want to work with you." And they did. They rerouted their road so it went away from the Iskut River and the salmon. They moved their tailings pond over here because people didn't want this lake to be damaged, but this valley was okay. They ended up spending several million dollars. Unfortunately, that project is mothballed now because gold prices have slumped. But, they worked so hard to get social licence from the communities, that we gave them a beaming letter of recommendation. So, we are not anti-development, by any means. Nobody here is. Most of the people opposing the Enbridge pipeline, would support a gold mine or a moly mine or whatever, in a heartbeat but coalbed methane and the Enbridge pipeline are going to impact our economy in a negative way.

*What does the future hold for SWCC?*

We had our heads down to solely focus on Shell in the Sacred Headwaters. We ignored everything else just so we could get that done. When we lifted our heads and took a look at what was going on, all of us at SWCC went through a little mini depression. In the upper Skeena up river of here, we have six pipeline proposals, two coal mines, a gold mine, a railway, a massive railway, road construction.

*So you can't stop, the struggle will continue?*

With all the major success we've had as a region fighting off fish farms, coal-bed methane, Enbridge, etc. has caused us to be classed as this anti-development region, which is so far from the truth. We have built our communities here on resource extraction. We are a pro-development region, through and through, and when you have 220 referrals going to one First Nation, that's more than the rest of B.C. put together.

*What do you mean by that?*

Two hundred and twenty referrals, so 220 mines, roads, power lines, oil and gas projects are being proposed in one territory, and that's just on Tahltan territory. There is so much being proposed that our bureaucrats in Smithers can't keep up. I have bureaucrats coming to me in confidence, in tears, because they didn't become scientists, they didn't go to work for the government so that they could become proponents for big industry. They are seeing their government, the government they work for, selling out.

The way I look at it is we have some really good projects being proposed. Some good projects and neutral projects and bad projects. Some super bad projects, and then there's these super duper bad ones. We can't even focus on a fraction of the super duper bad.

*I must ask you who coined that term, Sacred Headwaters?*

It's a translation of the word Klappan or Klabona.

*So, it's a literal translation?*

Well, there was some conversation about what Klappan or what Klabona means, and some people say it means Sacred Water and some people thought it meant where the water comes from. So, people just put the two together and called it Sacred Headwaters as the English translation. It came from the Tahltan.

*So, this region, does it connect with say opposition to KinderMorgan, opposition to Keystone, closing the Tar Sands, all of which are related to these bigger issues in the region, that of climate change?*

That's a good question, and I'm not entirely sure I have a very good answer for you. My personal view is that these pipelines are a joke. I mean they are not pipelines, they are spill lines. Every single one spills. It happens, and that's what history has taught us. And, my husband is a pipeline welder. I am a welder and I worked for a pipeline construction company building all the heavy-duty equipment that builds pipelines. Ditchers and side booms. I know the industry, and I know that fifty years from now, those pipes are going to leak. Yes, they will probably be pretty rock solid for the first decade and then you are going to run into all sorts of problems. So, that's my personal issue, or my personal opinion. But, from a regional perspective, there's really diverse opinions, and there are lots of people who don't want to see KinderMorgan go through because if there is a tanker spill in the southern coast, or when it comes through from the inside passage, that will impact us. And, the tankers are really big, even their name VLCCs, or very large crude carriers, showcase how massive these things are. They're out in the ocean and that's where our salmon grow and get fat. So, if we don't have the coast or the ocean in decent condition, then we are in trouble. So, we view these things as a direct threat to us. Some people talk about these things in war mentalities, not that they would ever be violent. But, they view these proposals as direct attacks on us. KinderMorgan is part of it because we've learned as a region how pipelines spill thanks to Enbridge. Now people have this broader awareness about what it means to have pipelines and it's actually educated the country, not just here. People are more educated and engaged here clearly, a vast majority, but I would say that it's applicable to all pipelines. We get it. Who would want to see a pipeline go through their community? But, how do we transport the very energy that we are absolutely dependent on, and it's a great question. I wonder if companies spent the same kind of money on alternative energies as they do developing oil whether would we all be in a better state.

*You've certainly been on an interesting journey, haven't you?*

Absolutely. My whole family. My father, who is a rodeo stock contractor, cowboy and logger for forty years, and guide outfitter, I mean he's on our board of directors. And, he is a huge advocate for us, he's where I get so much of my direction and perspective from, and Bruce Hill. I remember I went down to a conference, and I started talking about ecosystem-based management. Bruce said, "Quit talking like an environmentalist. You are not an environmentalist. The last thing this goddamn world needs is another environmentalist. They need somebody who is the cowgirl that you are. Don't start talking this eco bunk. Just say it how it is."

# ~ Roy Henry Vickers & John Olson ~

*Roy Henry Vickers was born in June 1946 in the village of Greenville, in northern British Columbia. Roy has stayed on the northwest coast of British Columbia ever since, residing at various times in Hazelton, Kitkatla, Tofino and Victoria. Roy's love of and respect for the magnificent natural beauty of this area is clearly evident in his art. His boldly colourful sunsets, subdued misty rivers and peaceful winter scenes reflect the essence of the west coast of Canada. Roy's father was a fisherman with the blood of three northwest coast First Nations, Tsimshian, Haida and Heiltsuk, flowing in his veins. Roy's mother was a schoolteacher whose parents had immigrated to Canada from England. This unusual mixed heritage has had a strong influence on Roy's art. Roy studied traditional First Nations art and design at the Gitanmaax School of Northwest Coast Indian Art in Hazelton.*

*Roy has received many awards and honours for his art and community involvement. Among them are a hereditary chieftainship and several hereditary names from Northwest Coast First Nations. In 1994, Maclean's magazine included Roy as the first artist ever in its Annual Honour Roll of Extraordinary Canadian Achievers. In 1998, the Province of British Columbia appointed Roy to the prestigious Order of B.C. and in 2003, Roy received the Queen's Golden Jubilee Medal. In 2003, a video featuring Roy was part of the successful Vancouver 2010 Olympic bid. In 1987, at the Commonwealth Summit in Vancouver, the original of Roy's painting A Meeting of Chiefs was the official gift of the Province of British Columbia to Queen Elizabeth II. Limited edition prints of the painting were presented to the forty-eight Commonwealth heads of state. During their Vancouver Summit in 1993, former Soviet leader Boris Yeltsin and former U.S. president Bill Clinton received artist's proofs of Roy's print The Homecoming as the province's official gift.*

*John Olson was born of Gitxsan and Carrier descent. From an early age his connection to the land was evident, as he crawled along hillsides picking berries with his grandmother, fished in his back yard along the mighty Skeena River and pushed his way to skinning his share of the moose at a young age. This connection to the land is a way of life for him and his family, a way of life that has to be protected.*

*We talked with Roy and John on the deck of Roy's house, with the Skeena River winding its way past.*

---

Could we start by you telling us how you became aware of the pipelines and what's happened since then?

(RHV) First of all my name is Roy Henry Vickers. I'm a member of the House of Qeel from Kispiox, I'm also a child of British Columbia. I've lived all over this province, and I've come back here to the banks of the Skeena River to live the rest of my life, and I'm living a dream. I grew up in Victoria from the age of sixteen to fifty-eight and always loved the north and thought of living here once again, so I'm living this dream on the banks of the Skeena River.

*When did you first hear about proposals for pipelines?*

(RHV) The Northern Gateway Pipeline? In December of 2011. A man by the name of Elmer Derrick, a person who was supposed to be working, or his title was one of the negotiators for land claims for the Gitxsan people, and all of a sudden in December, two years ago, we see it on the news that he signed an agreement with Enbridge on the Northern Gateway Pipeline, and that drove a number of people crazy. Because, first of all, he had no right to sign that. That was none of his business.

*So, who is he?*

(RHV) He's a member of the Gitxsan. He was rewarded by the government with a position on the Prince Rupert Port Authority. So, he is out of here all together. But, what Elmer did was he woke everybody up here. He woke us all up, and especially the young people.

*On what authority would he sign?*

(RHV) Nobody's authority. He said he was a hereditary chief, which is under dispute. So, he can say whatever he wants to Enbridge and they can say whatever they want about who he is in signing that piece of paper. He had no idea what giant he woke up. And, I was so excited to see us build a fire that stayed lit for weeks and weeks, twenty-four hours a day, young people coming out of the villages. All of the villages saying, "We've had enough of our hereditary chiefs telling us what we should be doing with the land. All they want is money, and the land is not theirs to accept money for. The land is theirs to be protecting for us and our children and our children that are yet to come. They have no right to be allowing a major pipeline to come through an area that will bring imminent danger to our land." And, that to me was the wonderful thing that happened in this nightmare. And so, that was my awakening, and it was a rude one. And so, here we are eighteen months or so later, I just wrote a piece on my Facebook page as a public figure in Canada.

*So, if you make us friends on your Facebook, we can access that?*

(RHV) Everything, yes. Roy Henry Vickers on Facebook is where most of my environmental political statements are made, you don't even have to friend me, you can just like it and you are there. Our ancestors are the land. When we allow some corporation to run a pipeline through this country for the promise of money, what we are doing is endangering what was left to us, and we do not have the right. Our own laws tell us we don't have the right to do that, and yet, there are people doing it. So, I'm not afraid to stand up and speak and say, "Look, you cannot sell it. You cannot. You don't have the right to. They can give you all the money they want to, but if the pipeline starts coming through here, we will be standing stopping the pipeline and we will die to stop the pipeline. It does not belong." I've said from the beginning, I would rather be a spirit than to see it go through. I feel that strongly that it doesn't belong here. There's another way. There's already a pipeline corridor to Kitimat, what the hell are they wanting to put it down the Babine, one of the most beautiful rivers, across the Skeena, across the Kispiox, which is world famous. Why do they want to do that? For money, but why can't they go where the corridor is already? It would cost them less.

The one place where they wanted to cross the Kispiox, the river does a hair pin bend and goes up and does another hair turn and then comes down and right where they want to cross it they would be crossing it three times. Three times! That's not going to make them money, that's going to cost them money. And, where they came out from under the river is in the flood zone of the river. So, the first big flood that the Kispiox has, the pipeline would get wiped out. They don't consult with anybody here. They consult with engineers who have no idea what they are talking about. They consult with marine engineers, who think that it's safe for massive super tankers to go down the Douglas Channel, and there are tug boat captains, professional tug boat captains who are non-Native who will tell you that an accident with a massive tanker of that size is imminent. It will happen in the first twelve months because it is a very tough passage. And the picture that they draw on their big commercial on the television is a lie. It doesn't even look like that. I've been there. I've been up and down there, and all of the turns and all of the islands that are there, they are not on their map. It's deceit and lies, and there are people here like me who have had enough. We've had enough of the lies, and so we will start talking. We will start screaming. We will start blocking.

*From our conversations, you are certainly not alone.*

(RHV) No. I know many. People will say to me, "Well, you can be bought out. And your people can be bought out." They cannot be bought out. It's priceless what you are talking about. It's not worthless, it's the opposite. They say, well what's the land worth anyways? It's not worth anything, the timber is all gone, fish are all gone. Well, you come and live here for twelve months and then tell me it's worthless. It's priceless.

*So, Enbridge and other companies are coming in and …*

(RHV) Buying whoever they can. Buying, and this is an old ploy. It's the government ploy, it was the church's ploy, it's the art collector's ploy. Art collectors who came into this country during the time when I was a boy. They would come into a village and see a priceless stone mask and they would try and buy it from the chief. Not for sale. Oh, I'll give you a lot of money. It's not for sale. Yes, but you must have a price? No, it's priceless. You cannot afford this. And so, what happens? A year later, the mask is gone. How did it go? They got somebody to get somebody to get somebody to go and steal it.

*That must be incredibly divisive and difficult for communities faced with these issues.*

(RHV) It is. You know, I came here nine years ago this past May 1, I came here from Tofino. I lived in Tofino from 1980 to 1995. When I got to Tofino I was a commercial fisherman. It was the end of commercial fishing, it was going fast. Why? Fish farms. There's major European corporations that have come in determined to wipe out all wild stocks of salmon so that commercial fish farms are viable, as far as I know. As long as we have wild fish, who wants to eat farmed fish? Not many people, well, nobody from around here will eat it. So, in Tofino, I built a gallery, and I began to make a living telling my stories in images. And, millions and millions of people over twenty-seven years, millions have been in that gallery. A whole industry. Many, many, families making a living from my gallery, from one person's art work. I came here saying, "Look, you think that the end of forestry means no more jobs here? You think that the end of commercial fishing means no more jobs here? What do you do for fun? You go up on that mountain with your ATV or you drift the river in a raft or you go fishing or you go cross country skiing. There are people who will come here and enjoy and pay you to enjoy what you enjoy. You have a whole industry here that you haven't looked at yet." I've been saying that for nine years, and gradually people are beginning to look at it and say, "Oh gee, we keep waiting for something to happen." Well, make it happen. And I'm trusting that us fighting pipelines coming across this country and people threatening open pit coal mining in the Skeena Headwaters will wake people up. People are beginning to realize, especially the young, that if we bring people here and we give them the experience, they will be our light in the darkness out there in the urban centres. They will be saying, "Look, you've got to go and see what's being threatened by our shares in whatever company or corporation." When people come and see this country they will, "Okay, this has to be protected."

*Are you referring to just the Enbridge pipeline or to LNG pipelines as well?*

(RHV) Any pipelines. I come from a little village on the coast called Kitkatla.

I have friends at Whale Point, and you can find them on Facebook, Whale Point, Hartley Bay, there are two biologists, who live there year-round and study the whales in Whale Channel. They will tell you of the danger to the entire whale population, all of the orcas, all of the remaining stocks of salmon if those super tankers are allowed in our inside passage. They do not belong there. So, if an LNG pipeline comes across here, well who is going to haul it away? Thousand-foot super tankers with sonars pinging off the bottom, day after day after day, 365 days a year, around the clock they've got to move. That will destroy the entire inside passage, which is one of the jewels in Beautiful British Columbia's crown of environment. They don't call it Beautiful B.C. for nothing. It is absolutely gorgeous. And those super tankers don't belong there. So, it doesn't matter what pipeline they want to bring through here, it doesn't belong here. Run it somewhere where you have already destroyed the land. The pipelines proposed will endanger one of the most beautiful remaining places left in North America, and people come from all over the United States, all over Europe to either fish in this river or to go skiing on our mountains. So, they know.

*It really doesn't make sense why they would do that.*

(RHV) Bob Dylan said it years ago, "It's law breakers making the rules." It's law breakers making them. Why? Because they want the money. Well, what do you want the money for? Is it going to buy back what you have destroyed? You can't buy back pristine country once it's destroyed. You can't fix it. Look at the Kalamazoo spill, and all of the insurance money that couldn't come close to fixing it. What did they do when they couldn't afford to clean up anymore? They covered it up.

*And called the clean up a major success.*

(RHV) Yes, and called it a success. And when people uncovered it and said, this is lies and deceit. What happened? They were gone after instead of the pipeline builders. Crazy, it's crazy. It's like people think we can fix everything and money will pay for whatever we want. It won't. And to me it's like, there are people up here who say, "It would be lovely if we had to go to our neighbours and trade them for some vegetables from their garden, and trade them some fish that we've caught. It would be wonderful if we had to go to our neighbours and say, could you guys come and help me? I just cut a bunch of timber here and I want to build a new house, and all the neighbours come over and they help build the house." That was life here. When I was a child, that was life here. Before welfare, everybody worked. Everybody worked. Everybody heated their house with wood and one of our jobs as children was to go out and cut the wood to heat the house. Now we have more and more efficient ways than burning wood to stop emitting dangerous gases into the atmosphere and people want to squash it. Why? Because they want us to burn oil. Well, oil is even more destructive, I don't know the whole scientific end of it, but I just learned in the last couple of days, about how the salmon, forty million salmon came back to the Fraser River a couple of years ago and nobody could figure out why, or at least they said they couldn't figure out why. I can't believe that fish biologists paid by the government didn't know why all of a sudden there were forty million salmon. It was because a volcano erupted and all of the dust and everything coming out of the volcano went over the ocean and dropped on to the ocean, and the iron in that dust started a plankton bloom, which all of the sockeye feed on. Sockeye feed differently than the other salmon. Other fish eat other fish, but sockeye eat plankton like whales. And so, all of a sudden there's this massive plankton bloom. What happens? There's this massive return of forty million sockeye to the Fraser River that's never seen that since, well, they're dead the people who used to see that. Nobody alive has ever seen that. So, excuse me, but if you now know the reason why, what are you doing to make sure that keeps going? Oh, well that would upset all the fish farms. Well, let's upset them then. Let's give healthier food to the people then.

*The Haida are trying that, aren't they, with these iron filings that they've been dumping into the ocean?*

(RHV) And they got jumped on. The powers that be brought division to the Haida community, and some of my friends were saying, we can't do that, that's genetic engineering. No it's not. It's doing exactly what Mother Nature has done for thousands of years, it's correcting what we are doing with fossil fuels and poisoning the atmosphere. The reason that there's no more iron going into the ocean is that the $CO_2$ emissions are so great the plants thrive and cover the land. The dust on the wind that use to blow out on the ocean and feed the plankton does not happen anymore. The plankton feeds the fish and the whales. All you need to do is stop our greenhouse affect, our gas, our fossil fuel emissions. That's all. Just stop it. Oh no, that will drive all the vehicle industry out of business. Well, let's drive them out of business then. Let's have electrical cars.

Feel that sunshine! In the north country here, we have sun, this birch tree won't grow on the coast because it's too wet. We have a lot of sun here all winter, when it's really cold and people down south say, "Well, how do you live up there in that cold north?" We live like you can't even believe.

*You are someone who has a national profile. So, why aren't politicians and others in power listening to the things that you are saying?*

(RHV) Many politicians, it seems, are influenced by the large corporations who have the money to be strongly influential. There are two local politicians who I've met and I believe they not only listen to us but they care about the environment and believe it needs to be protected. I will support these two by creating art work that will be sold and the monies go to supporting them. I will write a story that will be printed in papers and be available to the world via social media.

The reason why most politicians will not come to someone like me and have me speak for them and support them is because they are blind, blinded by money and the promise of jobs. They are the blind leaders leading the blind. And you've heard that story?

*Yes, I have.*

(RHV) You have taken a picture of the sweat lodge that I have built here. We have a teaching in the sweat lodge. There are four doors that we have, four times that we open the door and close the door, we sweat and pray and sing. The first door is for the teacher. Every teacher is a student. You as teachers, the more success that you have as a teacher will be governed by how much you continue to learn in your life. Nobody ever knows it all. So, you are a student your whole life. If you are a good student, you will always be a good teacher. If you love gaining knowledge, and the passion to learn, you inspire others to gain knowledge and that's who the good teacher is, not someone who just disseminates a bunch of information but someone who gives to children from their heart, from their spirit. So, the first door is a teacher.

The second door is the healer. When we gain the knowledge that we need healing, with that knowledge, we can take steps to heal. I need some healing in my life, then I go after the healing and it makes you a better person. That better person can see more clearly, that's the third door of the sweat lodge is the door of the visionary. So, you go from the teacher to the healer to the visionary. You cannot see clearly unless you have been through the door of healing. When all we have is knowledge and no healing, there's no heart, no spirit. Once the healing is there, vision will be clear. When our vision's clear, we are ready for the fourth door, the door of the leader. Then you will lead people and you will not be the blind leading the blind. If more politicians would go through the sweat lodge and understand in their mind and in their spirit, what it's about, they would be better leaders. They would not be bought by corporations. They couldn't be bought because the truth is the truth and the truth in us knows the truth in others. When you live in truth you will see the truth and know a lie when it comes. If you want to know the truth, you will know the truth, and the Christian Bible says, "The truth will give you freedom." And what is that freedom? That freedom is to stand as a warrior and a leader and say, "You are not being truthful to the people. So, can you please step aside. We want someone else in your place because you are not doing the job we want you to do." And so, once the people begin to heal and to see clearly, then they will demand better leadership in politicians. When that happens, things will change and people will listen to little guys like me.

*Even our provincial leaders at this point don't seem interested in listening even though there's so much opposition to the pipeline.*

(RHV) It's money, money, money. Addiction isn't just drugs and alcohol. Addiction can be money. When money becomes your addiction, that's all you think of. The only thing that you think is going to make you better is to get more money. That's the way people are thinking. What they don't understand is when you get old like me, you can't buy back your youth. There's no fountain of youth. When you lose a loved one, all the money, all the millions that you have cannot change that. When we lose that river, all the trillions of dollars cannot bring it back. Cannot fix it. When we think money can fix everything we believe a lie. It's just a fallacy. Money value rises and falls with the whim of whoever is playing the stock market.

What's real is the seasons and how much rain falls and how is the soil and are you looking after it properly or are you killing the soil because you are not taking care of it the way you should. The priceless things are the things that we are not paying attention to. First Nations people have interests in the land, but unfortunately for some it is changing from an interest to protect it to an interest to get money from it. It changed when welfare came to this country in 1958. I was a little boy. I was in Boy Scouts, and I've seen the change over the years, and people have become slaves to money instead of enjoying work, enjoying their family, enjoying the life that we live here. We don't have to live in the city, we don't have to go and get a job down there to enjoy our lives. My grandfather raised nine children and never went to school a day in his life. Raised them all successfully and loved them all. He didn't need schooling in a government school, he learned from the world around him, from nature. He didn't go to church, when I asked, "Where's your church?" He looked around at the trees, he looked everywhere, and then he looked at me and he said, "This is my church. This is sacred."

We've lost it, the connection to real time, to nature. We've lost it as a world community. For me, we are like what David Suzuki said, "We are in a vehicle going a hundred miles an hour headed for a brick wall and we are all arguing about where we are going to sit." That's the blind leading the blind. The driver is blind, he can't see the brick wall.

We have another opportunity for a revival of the human spirit, and it has nothing to do with religion. It's to do with our connection to the earth, our grounding to the earth, and what is that connection? It's knowing that that river rises and falls every year and the snow falls in the mountains and the snow comes down through the land and brings nutrients to the river and those nutrients go to the ocean and they feed the ocean, and then the ocean evaporates and goes up to those things and we call those big grey and white things "*yein*" in Gitxsan. The people here call that Yein, and we call that river Ksien and we call people GetKsien. Gitxsan, is now the way people spell it, but the old way of saying it was GetKsien. We are the people of that river, and that river is the juice from the clouds. And those clouds come from the ocean that that river feeds. So, it's all, the whole cycle is working, and when we interrupt the cycle, like we are doing, everything begins to implode, and it's time for people to wake up and smell the roses. You can smell them here. It's not just Alberta that is Wild Rose Country.

*It seems to me that the problem is the economic system, capitalism superimposed upon nature. As long as we believe in this system, unless you change or get rid of it, people can't smell the roses. They value money more than that. So, the problem is not so much money per se, but rather the system that makes people value money above all else.*

(RHV) Yes, and people say to me, well you are successful, you make a lot of money. Well, do you mean you don't value money? Well, I don't. It's just a tool. It's like my saw, it's like my ax. It's just a tool. It doesn't bring me happiness. The way I interact with my fellow man in this world is what brings me happiness. The way that I interact with that river and that tree and my land, that's what brings me happiness. You can't buy that, you've got to work for it. It's got to be a part of your being every day, and you can't buy it, you have to live it.

*Yes, in Bolivia, where the Indigenous communities, for the first time in history have actually gained state power to control their government, they are the government. They are talking about "living well," they are talking about an entirely different system and way of being, and in harmony with nature and solidarity with their fellow human beings. Certainly not the form of "development" that is promoted by many economists and others.*

(RHV) I carry a chief's name, Tlakwagila (Copper Man), and my responsibility to the name Tlakwagila is to be truthful, to serve the people, to give to the people, whatever I can give. John says there are sockeye running by here in a little while so I can catch sockeye in a net and can it all to preserve for the winter, instead, I pay someone from my village, Kitkatla, to can my salmon for me. Well, why would you do that when you have it for nothing here? Well, I share the wealth, I have the money, I can give it to her and she sells me the sockeye. It's okay. It's the way it should be to me.

People say you don't pay taxes because you live and you work on the reserve. I say, excuse me, you have no idea how much money I give to the community. How many times I give something to someone because they want to raise some funds. I give way more than the government would require from me in taxes. Someone else says to me, "Well, you guys all live off of us anyway. Off of our taxes. All the money you get from DIA [Department of Indian Affairs] is all from our taxes." No it's not. You don't have any idea where the money comes from, do you? The money comes from a trust fund that was set in place by the Crown when Canada was founded. All that we're getting on the reservations today is interest from that money that was set aside for us. The government makes the decisions as to how much money we are going to get. They pay millions and millions and millions of dollars to workers across this country who are non-Natives to be our caregivers. I don't need a caregiver. I can make my own decisions. If this community next door wanted me to be the chief counsellor there, not under the government's rule, but under their rules, the rules of our ancestors, I would go there and be their servant. I would go there and help them set up their business. I know how to run a business. I've had mine for twenty-seven successful years.

Nobody asks for help, yet the system is imploding. It's internalized colonization. We have those colonizers who came and brought genocide, cultural and physical genocide. There are children in graves in residential school lands that people don't even know they are buried there because they committed suicide in school. I know this because other children, my friends, had to bury them in the middle of winter. The world outside the reservations wonders what the hell is your problem? They have no idea, they don't even want to hear what the problem is when I start to tell them. How are we going to heal this? Can we heal this? Yes, we can. Well how? The first door, education. Help these people understand that it's not their fault. It's not their shame to be in the situation they are in, and bring them out of it, and when you do, you will see a healing spirit move across the country that this country has never seen, never. To me, those are the things that we should be thinking about. Not how to stop a pipeline. They will be stopped, but what do we do when that pipeline stops? What should we be doing? What is it that drives us to stop the pipeline? What is it? Well, it's heart. It's love. It's love of community. It's love of life. [His young daughter joins us]. Hey sweetheart! Speaking of love.

*Perfect timing.*

(RHV) Yes, and this is what we fight for.

(JO) Yes, absolutely. My name is John Olson, by the way, for the record, and I got involved in the resistance to the pipeline because on December 2, 2011, when that gentleman signed an agreement with Enbridge Northern Gateway on behalf of all Gitxsan people, it sickened me. I was physically sick.

When the Gitxsan people were in a court case, at the Supreme Court of

Canada, we were struggling. But the Gitxsan people reached out to our neighbouring nations, such as Haida, the the Haisla, the Talten, the Carrier and others, and they all came and gave us support. They helped us and showed their unity for our First Nations rights and by almost signing that Northern Enbridge Gateway Pipeline partnership deal on behalf of the Gitxsan, to me it is a great shame. It cast a great shame on the Gitxsan people. Because so many people were opposed to it, our neighbours. And, sure enough, the Carrier people, the Bear Lake, around Babine, they let out press releases and were upset.

It happened so fast. The reaction was "those sell outs" and we've got to do something fast here. So, we had meetings galore to select chiefs who did not agree with that partnership deal. But, you know, it did divide communities and family, the nation. And coming back to the money, the money is dividing people. I live off the land. I consider myself one of the wealthiest people because I have my berries, my smoked salmon. I had a whole elk brought right to my doorstep and given to me, and my friends looking out for me. So, I've got a lot of wealth, I guess, in that way. The grassroots people are the ones who are closer to the land.

*What's your view of the economic development and pipeline proposals being advocated for this area?*

(JO) It's just poorly managed and poorly thought out. Why make this happen today when we can take the time and thoroughly look at everything? To ship oil and gas to the coast or to another country in order to refine it and have it come back does not make sense. They will destroy what is left of the salmon, then we are going to be fighting over the water, and that's the actual water from around here. Just drank it, it's good water.

(RHV) Yes, my water comes from the river. So, the water you drink here is the river. How can that be? Well, it's filtered all the way to where my well is. I come home from the city. I run myself a bath and I climb into this bath and I say, "Oh, I'm so glad to be home." I can't even shower in the city water for more than 60 seconds. As fast as I can, I wash myself and get out of the shower because I'm allergic to chlorine. At home on the Skeena the water is good.

# ~ Murray Minchin ~

*Born in 1960, Murray moved to Kitimat in 1964. He began hiking at an early age and was allowed to camp alone in the forest and mountains starting at the age of thirteen. He attended post-secondary fine arts and photography schools. In 1992–93 he went on a six-month sea kayaking trip with his wife along the length of B.C.'s coast (two months in winter, two months in summer, two months in the fall) and produced a travelling exhibition using images taken with a 4x5 large format field camera. He worked at many different seasonal and contract jobs until joining Canada Post at the age of thirty-two. He has been working there for over twenty years, and is now coasting towards retirement as a letter carrier, feeling every subtle change in the seasons with nothing but the sky over his head. He was happily living life with his wife and their daughter until the threat of massive multiple-generation-lasting bitumen spills reared its ugly head in this place he loves and respects so deeply.*

*We met Murray in a parking lot overlooking Kitimat. He then drove us down to Kitimat Village, the primary residence of the Haisla First Nation and some dozen kilometres south of Kitimat. From there we walked out a short way along the rocky and driftwood strewn coastline to a spot where we could see much of the Douglas Channel. The interview represents his own personal views and not necessarily those of Douglas Channel Watch.*

---

*As we stand here looking out across the Douglas Channel, can you tell us the location of the proposed oil terminal?*

That's where the storage tanks are going to go on that low ridge over there. Because they haven't done a modern survey of the ocean floor for navigation hazards, they were running off the old information. They came up last year and they were doing a detailed survey of the bottom and they accidentally found a fifty kilometre fault line, right on the other side of those mountains, down the Douglas Channel.

*Can you tell us about your time with Douglas Channel Watch?*

When the Enbridge proposal first started to come out, my wife and my mother-in-law took notice. My mother-in-law was actually really active back in the day, when we were told that it was vital to the Canadian national interest that we have supertankers coming here, in the mid-seventies. Then they were going to build a pipeline to bring oil into Canada. That fell through for a number of reasons but then she got wind of this new proposal where we are now told that it's incredibly vital for our national interests that we get the oil going the other way. So she started researching it, and my wife started going to a couple meetings and they were coming back and telling stories about, "Well, they're going to bring supertankers in here." I was thinking, "Well, we have tankers coming in here but surely they're not talking about the big ones." And then I found out that they were thinking 525,000 barrels a day and then upping that to 850,000 barrels a day and having 1,100 foot supertankers zigzagging their way in here, 225 to start and then 360 plus once they get up to full capacity. That's when I became involved, when I realized that they weren't just talking about the regular coastal tankers that we normally get around here. Then the group itself got started. Dieter Wagner, who used to live here, and my mother-in-law, Margaret Ouwehand, Margaret Stenson and a couple of other people started the group, and then we went to a couple Enbridge-sponsored events.

*What year was that?*

That was three or four years ago, 2005 or 2006. It all started from that and we kept bumping into each other, all of us at the Enbridge-sponsored information sessions, which were scary and where we weren't getting answers. So we started to meet and met April MacLeod with the Kitimat Valley Naturalists; they had been an intervener in another project. She told us that "if you want to do anything, you should be an intervener, but you know, you really don't know what you're getting yourselves in for if you get involved." But we saw no option so we signed up as interveners and she was right. We had no idea what dedication and time sponge being an intervener would be. And how much research would have to go into it, but I'm sure glad we did.

*Research to make presentations to the JRP?*

Yes. In the beginning my thought was that if they're going to ram it through no matter what, then at least we're going to hold their feet to the fire and we're going to ensure that things are done as robustly as possible and to that end we have been successful. Because last year they found hundreds or extra millions of dollars for thicker pipe and more shut-off valves and people to man the pumping stations. And they heard that the public just doesn't trust them at all. So they started throwing in extra money and so we have been effective, not just us but all interveners have been really effective in that regard. But since then it's been one series of unfortunate events after another for Enbridge with the spill in Kalamazoo. And recently the National Energy Board found them in non-compliance for 117 out of 125 pumping stations for not having mandatory things like shut-off buttons and secondary power sources. So if Harper says yes and he tries to ram the project through, there's going to be so many people standing on the line, in front of bulldozers that the pipeline isn't going to happen.

*Do you think the federal government has any idea what they're up against in this particular project?*

Yes, I do. A year and a half ago I was an enemy of the state and a foreign-funded radical environmentalist. Joe Oliver was talking like that, Harper was talking like that. A perfect example of what British Columbians will do when they see their environment threatened is the Clayoquot Sound protest. It was the late seventies, early eighties. It was an isolated valley on the west coast of Vancouver Island. 10,000 people made their way out there to protest and over 800 got arrested. And that was before the Internet and social media.

*There is a history of resistance in this region as well, for example with the campaign for the Great Bear Rainforest.*

That was an interesting one. Have you heard of the baby buggy diplomacy and how that all came about? I think the one lady was the main activist to stop the logging and then there was a lady who was a head honcho of MacMillan Bloedel, I believe. And they met when they were pushing their baby buggies in Kitsilano; they met each other on a sidewalk and decided to go for coffee. And then they realized that there's a lot of forest out there that doesn't need to be clear-cut, it's not even marketable, it's small, scruffy, outer coast stuff. So they came to a balance, an agreement. They found that they could work together, get something that works for everybody, and then there were no big protests. Just happened on its own. But with pipelines it's all-or-nothing.

*I'm just wondering, in the case of the Enbridge project, is it the first time that you have seen a real coming-together of the Indigenous and environmental movements?*

Yes, absolutely. There's been a long history, perhaps going back to the Indian agents back in the day, of divisions between First Nations communities, but the Enbridge proposal has really brought a lot of people together in a way that hasn't happened before, especially with the oral statements. When people were speaking in Kitimat Village here, and the Aboriginal people got to hear about how much this place means to us, the newcomers, I think that was the first time that they'd ever really heard emotion like that from us, about how we love this place. And then we got to hear about things that I wasn't aware of. There are people here alive who remember living where the Alcan smelter now is and they didn't know anything was going on until barges turned up. So they were moved from that site, essentially a river was killed, and the valley cleaned out of timber in sixty years. So it was really an eye-opener for us too.

*What has Douglas Channel Watch specifically been doing in the campaign, what sort of activities have you been involved in?*

Well, I've got a life, so I limited my research and interest to where the pipeline comes out of the tunnels and all the geologic hazards and seismic hazards from there to here. Dave Shannon, he's a retired metallurgical engineer from Alcan who lives in Terrace and his area of interest was the marine aspects and the nature of double-hull tankers and how they're, from his perspective, just ticking time bombs because they're rotting from the inside out. There are three interveners in the JRP process, me and Dave and Cheryl Brown, who is more interested in some of the marine and social impacts. The three of us are independent but we work together as the Douglas Channel Watch group. The rest of the group are really active in support and organizing meetings and posters and bringing movies in for people to watch. They cover the activism part of it.

*It's very much a few people with common interests who come together.*

Yes, and talk about a wide spectrum too. Dieter Wagner, he's one of the first guys and he was a project manager at Alcan. Dave, he's a metallurgical engineer, he's an industry guy. People just from all over the map. The common thread being that we don't want to see this project in this place.

*Would you call this a citizen's coalition?*

Yes, for sure, and as grassroots as it gets and we were squeaky clean; we had no idea of what we were getting into and had never been involved in any project like this before.

*How do you coordinate with other groups like the Dogwood Initiative and the No Tankers campaign?*

My mother-in-law, Margaret Ouwehand, she's a hub and disseminates information out, so she is in touch with all those other groups. We keep in touch regularly. For example, there's a retired geomorphologist in Smithers, and Enbridge chose not to cross-examine him as a witness in the Prince George hearings. But then, in their final argument, they dragged him in the mud, and they contradicted what he said and they were questioning his qualifications. So I emailed Pat Moss today and asked "how can they do that?" Why not send a notice of motion into the panel saying that the proponent should be able to cross-examine the geomorphologist now, because Enbridge shouldn't be, or the proponent shouldn't be able to contradict or challenge somebody's evidence in the final argument when they had a chance to question him in the final hearings. I'm assuming they chose not to because he would have really damaged their case. So that's how we kind of look out for each other. That's one example of that.

*Have you been involved with the No Tankers campaign?*

Not really, no. I've been just blinders on in my little, little, tiny section. Otherwise you'd lose your life. It's just so big. At the final hearings I actually saw the proposal in the binders, they stretched easily from here to that rock. I don't know how many pages are in there.

*Over 7,000 pages, I think. So we are looking out on the Douglas Channel then?*

Yes, from those two points up this way is Kitimat. This is the top end of Douglas Channel with some 60 miles to open water. And there's two zigzag turns in narrow channels.

*So what happens if the tankers met each other in the middle of the channel?*

That's a good question. They say there's lots of room and Transport Canada has said that they don't need escort tugs and they don't need extra radar stations or anything. They're good to go right now.

*But what about the narrower points?*

Well, all the promises that Enbridge has made about tugs can be just smoke in the wind because Transport Canada says they don't have to use them.

*The No Tankers campaign is very big.*

In Vancouver, yes. And Margaret's really close with them but that's an aspect of Douglas Channel Watch I can't speak to.

*What about LNG and the proposed Kitimat terminal?*

My standard answer is that you'll have to go talk to the people where they're fracking, to see if they have a problem with it. But as far as from our perspective here, it comes with hundreds of jobs. If there's a break in the pipeline, it dissipates in the wind and it's lost profit for the company. There's no real environmental effect here and so the sense in the community is that they can take that. That might change once people find out how big the proposed Shell plant is.

*Is Shell doing the LNG plant here?*

Yes, just to the right of the wharf over there. It's a 48-inch diameter gas pipeline. And they, if they can't find power, electrical power to process the natural gas, then they'll have to burn off a percentage of it to run the refrigeration unit. And that, I've heard, would be the equivalent carbon footprint of a million people city. I don't know if that's true or not, but you can see the problem.

*If they have to burn the gas in order to liquify?*

And it's just a couple of kilometres to town.

*So it hasn't been decided yet, whether they'll have enough power or not?*

They haven't even formally submitted their proposal yet, so it's just another project at this stage. I'm not sure, there must be a forest fire down the channel because normally it's not this hazy. But with a plant like that the valley would be like this every day, whichever way the wind is blowing.

*What kind of process is involved in liquefying the gas?*

I've had blinders on for Enbridge, but as far as I know it's just a massive mind-boggling refrigeration unit so you can cool the gas down to minus 165 Celsius, where it turns into a liquid, then it's onto the ship and gone. That's what I believe is the process, but I'm not too familiar with it. It's a real energy hog for sure.

*Are the LNG tankers as big as the oil ones?*

Possibly, but what's funny about natural gas tankers is that they don't really get into that many accidents because when they do, or if they did, the people on board, if a fire got started, would be atomized. LNG tankers are typically owned by the gas companies, whereas oil tankers are generally leased and you're paying per day and the owner wants it now, and they take a lot more risks with oil tankers. And the number is a lot higher too so their frequency has an impact on the probability of spills and accidents.

*Will the same pipelines be used for gas and oil?*

That was part of our submission to the JRP. Since the omnibus bill C-38 and the changes Harper made then, I thought why not suggest to the panel that they might want to recommend that there be no liquid petroleum products crossing the north coast range, the north coast mountains on the north coast of British Columbia. So I asked them for a ban specifically because the natural gas lines can be switched over. Actually Enbridge is doing that right now, aren't they, to back east? They're reversing the flow, so part of our campaign is to get a ban on liquid petroleum products crossing the north coast, onto the north coast of B.C. That's the long game plan.

*Some people have said that the problem's not just the oil and the gas, it's the pipeline. Not just the construction but the corridor that it creates, because it really divides this territory into two. And if you have more than one, two corridors, however many, this will have large cumulative environmental impacts.*

That's a huge concern of ours in the Upper Kitimat River and the Hoult Creek valley where the tunnel is. It's really, really mountainous terrain and essentially the only flat part in the valley is the surface of the river and then it's only a couple hundred metres wide and then it goes up 5,500 feet from there. Starting at about a 20 degree angle going 30, 40 degrees and then steeper. The Pacific Trail Pipeline company is already in there, and they've already cut their right-of-way. Enbridge is planning on going uphill from that, so it's an angle about like this, that's very steep and they're going to cut a right of way for two pipelines. They have to cut into the bank and level it off and bury the pipeline. And it's really steep, lots of bedrock, it's really nasty country. So that's a huge concern for us, that's one of my biggest concerns.

One of our questions at the Prince George JRP hearing concerned the spill protection technology. With the pipeline alarm system, if it's tuned really, really, really finely, the alarms go off all the time. So you have to get it to a point where the alarms are only going off every once in a while. Each pipeline is different and that was one of our questions, and actually Sheila Leggett, the chair of the Joint Review Panel, asked for an undertaking from the panel themselves for Enbridge to explain this because the proposed pipeline route is going over the Rockies and then down and then over the bumpiness of the interior plateau and then up over the coast range and down again. What's that going to do to their spill detectors? What is going to be the minimum detectable spill amount?

*This certainly is a lovely spot.*

Yes, it's really nice when the whales come in, they've been coming in a lot the last few years, just grazing, they graze all the way up there and then they graze all the way back. Humpbacks. There's no salmon right now; our spring salmon are in but the real run is in the fall and then you get sea lions coming in and then they get the killer whales coming in.

*Are there any other problems that you foresee?*

Part of our final argument again was to ask the panel to recall John Cassidy, who's the head seismologist at Natural Resources Canada, because Enbridge of course decided not to question him. We are concerned about earthquakes in this area. As it turned out I couldn't make the JRP hearings that day so I left my questions with another intervener who then chose not to use them. So not one question was asked of the guy. There hasn't been a detailed study; well there's been no research in this valley essentially. I'm hoping that the JRP will call for a paleoseismological study. In the estuary, dig down through the peat moss and you look through the layers and you can see events that have happened, past tsunamis and events and earthquakes that have happened through the strata in the estuary, and above the estuary. So I'm hoping they do that.

*Are they doing soundings? I know there's a big issue in Atlantic Canada. They're doing a lot of sounding, and apparently there is a tremendous negative effects on the fisheries, and on whales, of increased shipping.*

No, they aren't, and I'm glad you brought that up because that's another thing that gives this project hardly any social licence in British Columbia at all. We have, since the late sixties, had a ban on all drilling or testing for the oil and gas that we know is out there. But British Columbians aren't willing to risk this for our own material enrichment and now, because Alberta has mismanaged their developemnt, and they're ramping up production, and it's got nowhere to go. And they're desperate now and Alberta's in debt even though it's supposed to be the economic engine of Canada. And so they're looking to us to shoulder all the risk to bail them out, when we're sitting on our own riches and we're unwilling to even explore for it. You've got me emotional on that one. They gave this no thought at all, it's a bunch of guys, like a bunch of eleven, twelve years old are going to build a fort down in the bush somewhere. "Let's build a fort!" You know, and they pick a valley that looks pretty good, and just, "Well, let's go! They'll love us there, we're going to bring fifty-two whole jobs." There's no thought that went into this at all.

Moreover, for whatever reason, the British stopped signing land treaties once they got up north on this side of the Rockies. So now the Aboriginal people have never negotiated their land, they've never given it up, they've never signed a treaty. So now each nation is a nation unto itself. And each nation could take it to the Supreme Court. I don't know what Harper was thinking at all, but he actually signed the United Nations Declaration for the Human Rights of Indigenous Peoples a couple years ago. Now he's painted himself in, in the world court. He signed, why he signed that, I have no idea. As soon as it was trotted out from the office, from the U.N., Canada should have been a signatory to that. But why he signed it now, I have no idea. I've heard industry insiders in Alberta calling the Enbridge project a dead man walking. And there's so many reasons why it shouldn't go. I'm really optimistic.

*What do you think the Enbridge people are thinking? They're getting all the heat. Do they finally know what they are up against?*

My standard line to that is they've bellied up to the trough so tight that it's cut off the oxygen to their brains. So they're missing it, absolutely. I'm not sure what they think.

*You could argue, for example, that Shell backed away from Sacred Headwaters because they were getting too much grief and was making it difficult to get what they wanted more, namely, LNG. So Enbridge could be in the position of finding that they just get so much negative publicity because of this, on top of everything else, that they might just come to some arrangement with the government in return for some other benefit.*

Yes, absolutely. And the harder Enbridge pushes, well it's like negotiating in any deal, if you like, the harder they push now and the more confident they appear and the more resources they put into it, it forces the government's hand and they'll get a better deal. I absolutely believe that they're white-knuckling it through this regulatory process waiting for another Plan B to get social licence. Apparently Irving Oil wants it and the Northwest Territories have said bring it on up.

*As you say the Northwest Territories has said, "Forget about B.C., send it up through us." Have the people that live there have any kind of contacts with you?*
     None.

*What's it like as an ordinary citizen, with no previous activist experience, appearing before the JRP?*
     Good, actually. When I first started my daughter was there in the public meetings. And my hand was shaking on the mic and I forced myself through the stuttering and everything. It's been a gradual thing. So, it's good and the format was structured in such a way that it absolutely just dove-tailed with the way I was gathering information because I would pull stuff from the proposal with the item number and linkages. And then put it into a separate text edit on the Mac, and so I had all that stuff there; all I had to do was just cobble it together with local knowledge questions and it worked really well for me.

*So they've created an activist in the process?*
     Pretty much. It's local knowledge that counts. The proponents don't have a clue what it's like here. A perfect example of that is in their final argument when they said that 97.8 percent of the centre line of the pipeline is within two miles of a road across British Columbia. We challenged them on that and said, "Well, how much of it is plowed in the wintertime?" We've had snow on the ground here for six months of the year before. So we asked how much is cleared in the wintertime and the answer is 28 percent. That's a big difference from 97 percent. And that's the local knowledge. It doesn't matter how many Ph.D.s and experts and witnesses they provide, we know what it's like here.

# ~ Des Nobels & Luanne Roth ~

*Des Nobels has lived for the past four decades on the north coast of British Columbia in the small fishing community of Dodge Cove, from which he fished commercially for almost thirty years. He is a keen advocate of the marine environment and the people and communities that rely upon it, and he continues to do so through the T. Buck Suzuki Environmental Foundation, where he has worked for the last nine years.*

*Luanne Roth worked for a decade in the eighties with Greenpeace Canada, rising to the position of CEO. She felt the call of motherhood and the ocean and left Vancouver to have a child and be immersed in the coastal environment and communities she loved and worked to protect. She and her husband found time to be involved in local environmental issues and enjoy the coast, building a small-boat, family fishing business out of Prince Rupert.*

*She recently joined the T. Buck Suzuki Environmental Foundation as northcoast energy campaigner. She still retains her volunteer position as marine director of Prince Rupert Environmental Society and its Save our Skeena Salmon campaigns, through which she edited the coastal community anti-tanker book* The Salmon Recipes, *and in the past helped win a moratorium on salmon fish farms on the north coast. She has also served as a board member of Friends of Wild Salmon and Skeena Watershed Initiative.*

*We met with Des and Luanne in the T. Buck Suzuki office in downtown Prince Rupert, a modest room upstairs in a building also housing the United Fishermen and Allied Workers' Union. The words and thoughts contained herein are solely theirs and do not necessarily reflect the views of the organizations for which they work. We each bought copies of* The Salmon Recipes *and highly recommend it. You can get yours at http://saveourskeenasalmon.org/.*

---

*As someone who has spent of good part of your life in the commercial fishery, the case against oil pipelines and tankers here must be obvious enough.*

(DN) We have had the one good stroke of luck in having an abundance of wild salmon within this region, and an abundance of people who earn their living from or continue to take some of their livelihood from fish. That has been the one galvanizing issue through this region and will continue to be a galvanizing issue for as long as they're destroying salmon.

They are working very hard at that, unfortunately, and I would liken it in many respects to a place in the prairies in the late 1800s, with respect to the buffalo and colonization. It's not a lot different, as long as buffalo existed, people had something that they felt that they could rely upon. And therefore they were not all that interested in adopting things that really weren't in their nature. Same thing here, and as the fish are diminishing, as they continue to reduce in volume, that ability to confront and try to protect diminishes as well. That's sort of what you're seeing. Luckily, those people that are not involved in the fishery do have a fairly close connection, and then there's a strong First Nations involvement through the region as well. Although I would suggest that that's beginning to waver. It's been roughly fifteen to eighteen years since they began to really downsize the fishery here and restrict opportunities, that sort of thing. And we were already fairly depressed at that point, going from a town that was very wealthy to be perfectly honest, people did well, they lived well. And there was very little disparity across the racial communities and the various groups, but if you starve people long enough, shit tastes good. And they brought a whole lot of shit, to be perfectly honest, and people are starting to get a taste for it, because there's been nothing else for a long time. And so they are grasping at things that may allow them or their children to remain in some fashion. But what they're finding though is that in many cases, their children are still having to leave here. These new projects don't provide long-term sustainable jobs or communities. They don't benefit or create community structure, they don't support any of that. And in the end what they bring is a very short-term bit of money and after they leave we usually end up with all the garbage they leave behind. There's no real effort to clean these things up. We're still cleaning up mine sites from forty, fifty years ago at the taxpayers' expense. I'm a real pessimist to be perfectly honest. I've been at this too long to really feel very optimistic anymore.

*Do you think that the unintended consequence of Enbridge has been the galvanizing of support across the region?*

(DN) There's always a possibility of that. But many of the groups that are involved in this have been involved previously in a range of issues and will probably continue to be so. One of the things that many of us are starting to come up against now though is that the funding that previously existed, that allowed us to at least form some sort of front to these various projects or at least respond to them in some fashion, is disappearing.

*So you used to get federal government money or you could apply for various programs?*

(DN) No, just grants from various organizations, nationally, and those are drying up very quickly. Our present government has done a very good job of witch-hunting and creating an immense fear. And that includes going after the major funders, and it has put the scare, unfortunately, into the environmental community.

*There's been a big chill as a result of the clampdown on political advocacy?*

(DN) Yes, we're beginning to live in what I term a police state, a totalitarian state, a very fascist looking government at present, and I don't foresee any let-up on their side in terms of development projects. They're driving anything and everything they can as quickly as possible. Despite the fact that LNG really has no market. For years we subsidized all the coal out of here to Japan. You know, we paid close to 60 dollars a ton, Canadian taxpayers did, to ship it to Japan. We built this port, now the federal government wants to sell it. Sell it to the Americans so they can pump out their coal over to China as well. Everybody says, "Well, China's going to be green in six years." So why are we doing all this, what is all this about?

*This whole extractivism model is certainly a development trap. The same thing with Enbridge. I think it's great to bring people together in resistance to this pipeline. Your question is what happens after — or instead of — Enbridge. Can we have community-based resource development?*

(DN) I should guess not, not in light of the two governments we're dealing with, both provincially and federally. They've been emboldened by the majorities that they've achieved, despite the fact that it's been a very small part of the populous actually voting. But they're quite emboldened, and industry of course is backing them to the hilt.

*But it is interesting to at least wonder if people will come together not only in resistance but in doing something about it. Not leaving it to governments to support this or that activity, but might this galvanize possibly some kind of collective or community-based action to do something? Just to preserve this, the watershed, salmon and so on, a way of life? To recognize that in order to preserve the way of life, the livelihoods, they have to do something. They can't simply react to these companies doing all these things.*

(DN) To that end, a number of things have been tried. We've spent inordinate amounts of time in devising methodologies that would give government what they're looking for and still provide us an opportunity to generate an income and maintain a resource base.

*Like what, for example?*

(DN) Well, and this is outside of particularly Enbridge, I have worked a lot with the fisherman's union and we have spent the last two and a half years forming a group called the Sustainable Marine Fisheries and Communities Alliance. And this is all First Nations communities, all non-First Nations communities and the fishing interests coming together and devising a scenario of monitoring and enforcement initiatives that would allow us to carry on fishing. Much of the fishery that we don't participate in anymore is because the Department of Fisheries and Oceans

(DFO) doesn't have the management capability, so in its wisdom it shuts fisheries down, it's not a conservation issue, it's no other reason other than they don't have the money or the people to put on the ground. Therefore they can't monitor the fishery; therefore they don't open it. All of our communities lose, so we put together a very comprehensive monitoring program; we had a supplier who would supply the monitors and all sorts of things. We went to the department, brought it to them. "Can't be done, can't be done, you have to use this provider over here, you have to do this you have to do that", we were told. We're going, "Why? We've met all of your requirements? Everything is done here, this saves us money and allows the fishery to carry on and you continue to put roadblocks in front of us." Every time we've come up with or devised a method that would provide them their needs and still allow us to fish, it just keeps getting knocked down. And we've done this time after time, from gear changes to fishing times to all sorts of restrictions we've placed on ourselves to try and maintain some sort of fishery. We've done everything and we've got nothing.

*You don't see any possibilities for some kind of community-based resource management or community resource management structure?*

(DN) Oh definitely. I mean First Nations are madly working to try and do that. We've had two processes, we're in the midst of the MaPP process right now, which is a marine planning partnership. We've delivered the PNCIMA process — the Pacific North Coast Integrated Management Area — of the Department of Fisheries and Oceans under their new Oceans Act four years ago. "Thou shalt do this," we all bought into it, said great, this is supposed to be a collaborative governance structure, we will devise an integrated management plan that will allow all of us to operate. The shipping agencies went to Ottawa and said, "You can't let this go ahead. This is going to kill us." They killed the process. That was the end of it — we got the third draft, just came out to go on the shelf, never be seen again. MaPP is a process that's between the province and First Nations, which came out of PNCIMA when the process fell apart because they felt they still needed to carry forward with some issues. Again, we tried to work very closely with those groups, trying to create the capacity here, in terms of monitoring and enforcements. We're not getting opportunities, we're not allowed to do these things, or if we do get anywhere, they start providing us with more roadblocks as we move forward to the point where something that was very simple, it was very cost-effective, all of a sudden it becomes ridiculously complicated and over-expensive.

(LR) Another reason that the coastal fishing communities can't stand up to the government is that they don't have public support. I think there has been a very sophisticated international effort over the last two decades to prepare the area for oil and gas. Each time the oil and gas industry has tried to come into the region before, the fishermen were the backbone of the opposition which kept them out. The industry has learned from past attempts. They have very deep pockets, and I think they use their charitable arms to fund groups that are divisive, that hurt the fishery, that remove fishermen from the coastal waters and weaken the community.

(DN) You're quite correct, I mean, some of the groups that we have to work with against the oil companies were groups that we fought with for many years. Because they wanted our commercial fishery gone.

*So recreational and commercial fisheries are coming together over this now?*

(DN) What we've done is we've agreed to set those things aside while we fight this battle which will kill both of us. It's, "My enemy's enemy is my friend." That's the premise under which we're really operating at present, but there's not a lot of love lost between a number of the groups. We're together because we have a common goal.

(LR) But the damage has been done. The fishermen here can't go to the public, can't go to the Canadian public and fight for the resource and fight to keep fisheries going because they've effectively had their reputation totally trashed in the media by some environmental groups and the sports fishermen. Unfairly I think. In the eighties people used to worry that the main threat to the marine environment was pollution from the oil industry, but for the last couple of decades they have had their gaze directed onto fishing. The funding for that shift has come in large part from the oil industry. People think the B.C. coast is poorly managed and fished out. They have no idea that about 200 million kg of wild capture seafood comes from it sustainably, every year — it is rich. If they do happen to hear about a good catch it is described in terms like "lucrative fishery". The fishing community is almost always described in negative terms: they are greedy or they don't care about the environment, or they are too ignorant to understand sustainable management. I remember one big environmental meeting about marine management in B.C. was advertised with a poster calling the ocean a crime scene and one of the academics on the panel called fishermen "roving bandits".

It is impossible to defend against in public, but I live in Rupert and I know the fishermen who are being attacked. More than half the fishermen are First Nations and many of the commercial fishing industry leaders and spokespeople are also highly regarded chiefs and community leaders. And the other fishermen as well are often highly intelligent and knowledgeable, third and fourth generation, bound to the community and deeply caring about the ecosystem and longterm sustainability. These were the leaders who were out with their fathers in boats to protest the proposed Kitimat oil pipeline in the late seventies.

I don't know why the industry is so denigrated but it is. So that now when the seafood resource needs champions to stand up for it and we need our fishermen to stand up for this important Canadian resource, they are crippled. What is the main industry that is standing in opposition to B.C. offshore oil and gas? What is the main value for Canadians that's at risk from tankers there? It is the fish, the resource of these fish. And yet, the resource and the people have been totally belittled. I remember an article in the *Globe and Mail* about fish being worth pennies per pound. Well, maybe our pink salmon sell for pennies, wholesale off the seine boats but they're still valuable as a healthy food, loaded with omega-3. Or an article saying, "Oh it's all exported anyways". Well normally if we have export dollars coming into Canada, that's something we think is great.

Whatever is causing it, it has been huge. Fishermen can do nothing right, and policy after policy results in less fishing even in the face of strong stocks. I can't help thinking there is a government policy to make way for oil and gas and that the people in non-governmental organizations have their perceptions influenced by where oil industry charitable arm funding is going; any grant proposal which might lead to a reduction in the number of fishermen gets funded. For instance, monitoring programs were set up in a way that wiped out about two-thirds of the small-boat fleet in the groundfishery. The smallest, most environmentally sustainable, were hit the hardest. These kinds of initiatives get funded and, inadvertently I think, a lot of well-meaning people, cause harm. In other parts of the world people are starting to question the MSC sustainable fish certification because of the effect on small boats and many other countries have put in special policies to protect their small-boat fleets. But here in B.C., even after the groundfish fiasco, we have many environmental groups pushing for electronic monitoring on the smallboat gillnet fleet, which is half First Nations, tied to the communities, caring of the fish and they can't possibly afford thousands of dollars each annually for this program. We are going to wipe them out too.

*Obviously the tensions between commercial and recreational fishers, between labour and environmental interests, have led to many divisions which are difficult to bridge even with the pressure of a large external threat such as oil pipelines and tankers.*

(DN) We should give you a bit of background about our organization. T. Buck Suzuki is an environmental foundation, we are an environmental organization, formed in 1981. We actually predate most of the environmental movements in this country. The reason it was formed is because commercial fishermen decided it was time to fight these kinds of industrial expansion. Fraser stocks were in threat, there's a range of things that were being developed. And we as fishermen know the need to protect habitat, we know the need for cold water rivers to make sure that our fish don't die within the systems. So this organization was formed to represent the interests of commercial fishermen on the environmental front. And that's where we come from so you'll hear us talking about commercial fishermen a fair bit, and it's because these are own constituents, and they are environmentalists. They were the first environmentalists. That being said, because of our close connection to the industry, we've been shunned by the majority of environmental organizations. We are not invited to the marine stewardship councils; we are not invited to many things that the environmental movement is active on because of our affiliation with the fishing industry. Which I think is rather foolish on their part.

(LR) It is hard for us to talk about because everyone assumes we are biased and speak out of self interest, but I don't even fish Skeena salmon. But it is mostly fishermen that know what is going on. I fish groundfish and sometimes catch Columbia salmon off Haida Gwaii with hook and line. My interest isn't personal financial, it is because I live here and I see what is happening. I was an environmentalist working for Greenpeace before I was a fisherman. The public perception of gillnet fishermen is so bad I know I am nuts to defend them. I only hurt my own credibility but I don't care. Lately, I wanted to learn more so I really got involved and started going to Skeena fisheries meetings, and I think they are being shut down unnecessarily.

Another policy which has reduced the number of fishermen on the coast was the result of arguing that the sports fishery is more valuable than the commercial fishery so we should cut back the commercial catch. Most of the arguments I have seen to support this compare the commercial wholesale value to the sports retail value. Well the government economists aren't that stupid. Why would they accept such flawed argument unless they had an overriding policy like oil and gas. Get rid of the people who live in and are tied to the community and encourage tourists. I was involved in an economic report about the comparable value of the sports and commercial fishery on the Skeena and was allowed some input so I put in a request that we compare retail to retail value. The report showed the Skeena was worth about $110 million — $83 million commercial and $15 million sports and some other stuff. Years later, after a policy to reduce fishing on commercial stocks to save steelhead, the commercial revenue was down by tens of millions and the sports was still around $15 or $16 million.

I really wanted to know if this was the result of stock declines, so I got involved in going to some of these Skeena fisheries meetings. I don't think it is the stocks — when the stocks are the same the amount that's being allowed to be caught has gone down to what, 30 percent, 20 percent.

(DN) No, we're fishing at below 20 percent.

(LR) This is really important for the Enbridge tanker issue. The oil and gas industry has wanted into the west coast for decades. This is an ongoing struggle between the people who live here and have access to the marine resources now (the fish), and the industry, which wants in either for tanker traffic or offshore drilling. The government is on the oil industry side and they implement policies to weaken us. How else can you explain the upriver policy? You just have to go back to the Cohen commission if you want an unbiased view. The Cohen commission is the one into the millions of Fraser sockeye which went missing, but he looked into other management issues as well. The media hasn't covered it, but in his report, he came out against the upriver fishery policy of DFO. Everyone has been told and all the big environmental groups say that for conservation reasons, to avoid mixed stock weak runs, we should fish upriver, but there is no science to support it. I asked one of the local First Nations fisheries officers if he was worried that fishing in the main stem of the river might sometimes hit some schooling weak run far harder than any ocean fishery, where the stocks aren't schooling, and he said he was really worried about it. Think about it, most of the weak stocks are the furthest up, from the spawning streams furthest inland, so as you move the fishery further upriver you target them harder and harder.

And even more important, salmon quit eating in the ocean and use up their oil reserves to swim upriver, and their oil reserves are lost first out of their muscle; their filet, so, the loss in food value is huge. The value of upriver fish is about a tenth. So it's basically a destruction of the fishery, right. Of that whole fishery, it's huge, you know, it's a huge, huge issue to move it upriver like that. Take our main fishery and destroy it to a tenth of its value. How can coastal people have the strength to fight the oil industry? And Cohen came out and said he couldn't see any conservation argument for it.

*Have there been any studies of this whole dynamic?*

(DN) We have just completed a very comprehensive socio-economic study of the impact of the fishery to "community". What it looks at is not the ex-vessel price of the value of fish, but the actual community fabric that revolves around the catching, supplying, processing and consumption of fish, the intangables.

*Is the study available?*

(DN) We had it done to augment the marine planning process, to inform the marine planning process because we get all these economic studies, purely neo-classical economics. Dollar in, dollar out, that's it. No concept of how this builds community, how things are tied. So we felt we should do this. The problem is that the marine caucus, which was part of the marine planning process has withdrawn from the process because the feds are not at the table and there's no way of discussing fisheries with only the province. There's no jurisdiction. So that being said, the document which was created for them is in their hands. We're going to have to have a discussion with them. We set it up, we did the work to produce it, but it belongs to them.

*You mentioned the community-based nature and impacts of the industry. Is that how you see it?*

(DN) Yes, our fishery has always been portrayed as an industrial complex, but it's not. There are the Jimmy Pattisons, there are a few of those large players. But for the most part we are small owner-operators, family operations. That's a very different thing, some of the environmental groups, we finally managed to convince them, "Listen, you're killing off small people here, not killing off a large industrial entity, if you think that's what you're doing." And they began to understand that. The problem is they had already started a process that was snow-balling and there was no way that they could stop it. So we're still portrayed as this industrial complex. So now they think the transferability of quotas is a good thing because it'll reduce the number of vessels. What they don't understand is it really concentrates the holdings within the large industrial fishery that didn't exist before.

(LR) One of the things I see as positive is the slow food movement and the interest in food security. That's what we're trying to connect with in our book *The Salmon Recipes*. This book has stories from the Enbridge coastal hearings. People are explaining who they are and how they are connected to the salmon and the sea. I hope the book helps start moving people through to kind of see fishermen as, you know, like they do organic farmers. See that Enbridge is threatening ordinary caring people who are producing sustainable food, for them. We wrote this book partially to tell the story of the importance of the marine resources for the First Nations culture but also to show Canadians that it is important to them too — a significant national food supply. The book is just a happy celebration of our recipes and our culture here on the west coast in the north. Help everyone understand it has real value.

*How many companies are operating in the commercial fishery here now?*

(DN) Mainly one company, Canadian Fish. The rest are custom processors, where they do virtually nothing but offload fish at the station and ship it down south to a non-unionized plant where they hire Filipino, Vietnamese women who they can browbeat. Now, they're shipping over to China to be processed, the fish goes into a container, gets refrigerated, goes over to China, gets processed, gets shipped back to Canada, and then goes into the retail stores.

(LR) There are some smaller plants still processing, like Aero Trading and CB

Isle. The Lax Kwa'laams First Nation has reopened their plant and is now doing groundfish as well as salmon

*What has been the position of the fishermen's union on fish farming?*
(DN) Fin fish or shell fish?

*Both.*
(DN) We adamantly oppose fin fish. We fought it long and hard here. We have a moratorium in place in the north coast, on the basis of that battle. In terms of shellfish, we're very supportive. We're talking scallops, oysters, mussels, that sort of thing. Shrimp, no. There's no place to raise shrimp here. We have very large wild shrimp populations, it's not an issue. Our problem with shrimp here is market. Getting it to. We're in a place where you have a hard time getting things out and we don't have a large enough local market to warrant selling into the local market. So it's restricted, but we have a very strong shrimp stock out here. Problem again is the DFO has overloaded those guys with huge amounts of costs to go and fish. Most businesses have the ability to pass on costs to the consumer. Commercial fisherman doesn't, neither does a farmer. These guys are getting paid for their fish right now what I got paid thirty years ago. The only difference is that the cost has gone up a hundred fold, and so that's why they can't survive. They cannot live on a $1.25 a pound for fish. In Alaska, you've got plants up there and they take more of our fish than we take here. We reduce for conservation, they up their catch. And they've told us for years, if you guys won't catch them, we will. And they watch us, and they go, "You're idiots." You can see them right across the line, we fish within a quarter mile of each other, those guys fish for six days a week on that side of the line, we fish for sixteen hours a week on this side. They catch 300,000 chums on that side on the line, we're allowed 10,000 chums.

(LR) We've got such a huge resource and so much opportunity here; it's really just been pushed down.

*Do you think that one day they will get rid of the moratorium on oil and gas explora-tion around here?*
(DN) Yes.

(LR) I am worried all this push for LNG is another step closer to offshore drilling. I think as long as the fish are here we can turn things around, and more and more people are starting to catch on. Some fisheries scientists are starting to question DFOs new management. But we really need to wake up and change things.

(DN) There's no reason for this town to really exist here anymore. We've had six years of this new port development and half of our downtown is still closed up, locked down tight and will remain so. This LNG will do the same thing, camps come in, camps leave. They don't need this town here, it has no reason to be. The only reason it was here was because of fish and trees. One time under the adjacency and appurtinancy clause that government used to enforce, we had a percentage of the wood and fish that was processed here. But once they'd removed that, we have no reason to exist, and if you break people from their connection to the land and water, to the resource base, they no longer care about the resource, and they move on. There's no tie to place, there's no tie to anything. What industry and government have created is these migrant work forces that they shift to wherever they think they need them for whatever purpose but they don't want them fixed anywhere where they could grow an attachment to and actually feel for. That's not in their interest.

(LR) This river, the Skeena, is the second largest salmon river in Canada. And its estuary is right where they want all this industry to go, so it's really a problem. On the one hand we could have a long-term sustainable industry which provides healthy food for millions and thousands of jobs for locals. We are losing that to let in an industry that provides huge profit for investors, but it is only for the short term and then only for the few.

(DN) The Department of Fisheries and Oceans, all of their work that they did in the mid to late eighties around the development of the Port of Prince Rupert, told me very clearly, that the area of Lelu island and Flora Banks was a no-go area, you do not develop here. Those reports were shelved and never looked at again. They don't even exist in the minds of all the developers or in terms of the federal government. We've had to dig them back out and submit them to government as evidence. Stating, your own people have said this should not take place. We have huge tracks of land not far away that are suitable, that could be used, and we wouldn't necessarily oppose there, but we're gonna oppose it here and we're gonna fight them tooth and goddamn nail. Because they're gonna kill it. They don't care. The government of Canada gave the port land that's within a conservancy to develop. What the hell is this government doing?

(LR) The port can coexist with the salmon; the grain terminal is okay, the container terminal, lots of it is fine but now suddenly they want to put a trestle across a critical eelgrass bed, one that is crucial to the Skeena salmon and has been recognized in the past as needing protection. And we are concerned they are going to put in a pipeline for tarsands bitumen under the sheep's clothing of a natural gas pipeline — the pipes are identical and have been switched in other places.

*Is the fishermen's union opposed to LNG?*

(DN) Not LNG per se but particular LNG projects and the placement of them. We have some concern over the scope and the scale of what's being proposed. To be perfectly honest anyone I've talked to thinks this is ridiculous, this is not going to happen. It's purely speculative.

*Most of the projects are not going to happen?*

(DN) No. There's ten proposed for the north coast. Out of that ten, two will probably get developed. And one might actually get into China. Indonesia and Australia right now, they're already at the front door. They're developed, they're in. They're going to produce everything. The Chinese are madly learning all of our fracking techniques. They're going to be going into their coal fields shortly and they will not need any natural gas at all. So what are we doing this for, for how long, and what are we left with in the end? A destroyed river, a pile of useless infrastructure and a mess that we end up paying as taxpayers to clean up.

*Sounds like 'development'!*

(DN) Yes, it does, doesn't it. Sounds like business at any cost. The sad part is that, even in terms of what's expected by government from industry, in terms of remediation, end of life, for these sites, is minimal. There is a small portion at the end of these environmental assessments, when they apply for them, stating that they will remediate at the end of the project, based upon the required regulations at the time. But there's no bond required up front. If you and I go rent an apartment, you pay a damage deposit up front, it's very simple. Our government hands over huge tracts of land and incalculable wealth to idiots that walk away and leave us with a mess. There's something very wrong with that. There's no due diligence on the part of government. I would characterize that as negligent. We have a government that right now in my mind that is treasonous to this country.

*Luanne, you're not with the union?*

(LR) No, and I only just started with T. Buck a few months ago. My main work in opposition to Enbridge was as a volunteer, just like the majority of people. But the fishermen's union is one of the important parts of the environmental movement here; they are one of several longstanding structures which help organize. On the coast they are mainly the First Nations bands, the fishermen's union, the Prince Rupert Environmental Society and the T. Buck Environmental Foundation, and upriver there are the sports fishing orgs and Northwest Institute, and we have a group where some of us come together for some projects (Friends of Wild Salmon).

Saveourskeenasalmon.org is a website where people can buy *The Salmon Recipes.* I'll explain how that book fits into the movement. One of the main actions to fight Enbridge was the thousands of people who spoke up at the hearings. It was an almost 100 percent volunteer effort, but the union and T. Buck and FOWs all really helped by letting people know about timing and procedure. After the hearings there was just a big groundswell of grassroots people wanting to keep up the pressure and eighty people in Rupert formed an ad hoc group. Their main project was the creation of a book giving the coastal side of the issue. It was intended as a gentle beautiful gift to people, with great salmon recipes, to teach them about the value of the clean ecosystem to the salmon and people. It drew on the testimonies. It was another 100 percent volunteer project, but it needed structure so it used the Prince Rupert Environmental Society, who were well known and trusted and offered to oversee, use their bank account and non-profit status.

(DN) This website was initially set up when we were dealing with the salmon farm issue.

*Do you see yourselves as part of the "environmental movement"?*

(LR) No, I feel myself more of a north coast community of people.

(DN) With an environmental bent.

(LR) Yes, we care about the environment.

(DN) We care about the environment, we care about our place.

(LR) And sustainability.

(DN) We're accidental environmentalists.

(LR) We feel like we're part of the environment, I think that's the difference.

(DN) We have an understanding of our place within the environment, as opposed to really being separate from it. And as such we know the place, we feel for the place and protecting it, we get branded as environmentalists. But we're not, we're just people that love this place and love what it provides and people are destroying this. For what?

(LR) So I do see myself as an environmentalist in that regard.

(DN) I never considered myself an environmentalist. People have called me that, and I've said, "I'm not an environmentalist, I'm a humanist." I believe in humans and I'd like to see us continue to exist on this planet. Another question is what are we going to do about it? We're the problem, not the planet. It doesn't need saving, it's going to be here after we're gone.

(LR) Years ago I would have proudly claimed myself as an environmentalist but lately I have been ashamed at some of the statements coming from the mainstream, outside-funded, ENGOs. They show no respect for the local people and no understanding of the issues. When you have on one side First Nations leaders and other community leaders who have been in the fishing industry for generations, who know more about the salmon — individual runs and timing and care about their long-term health and care about their communities. And you have on the other side some young out-of-school environmentalists or biologists saying they should be monitored and their recommendations shouldn't be listened to and that they are greedy, ignorant, wasteful and don't care about the fish. Well I know who I trust and who I respect.

I think you came here thinking how the broad movement against Enbridge would bring us all together, and it has locally. The effort so far has really strengthened connections between people. But what we have been describing to you is that the movement needs to be a lot smarter and that overall we have lost ground since the eighties. There are forces at play which are dividing us. I have hope because the true basic values — caring for each other, having clean healthy food and water — these values keep coming out. But it is hard in the face of the sheer power of the industry and its short-term wealth. There are a lot of local people and groups, they cover the whole range — teachers, politicians, young people — there's the whole range working here to keep our coast but it's hard. There are small capitalists who love the system, who vote Conservative, who just say, "Oh, this is a mistake." They still think that we have to stop Enbridge. It's a real range I must say.

(DN) And that's been the interesting thing over the years is the maintenance of this coalition, over time, through a range of events and issues. It hasn't just been one. It's been one after the other and we've been extremely successful in either sidelining the worst projects or stalling them in sufficient fashion that they don't come about, so there is that ability. People have been empowered by that and continue to come together over these issues. We have quite extensive discussions as to where we go next. Is there something that we're facing that might be worth taking on? Is there something that is of concern to someone that, you know, should we be looking at this? And we've always agreed that we'll look at one issue at a time as a coalition. And when we've dealt with that, we'll look at something else possibly or we may dissolve. There's never been any guarantee of beyond this point.

One of the things about today's society is the way that we have structured our economic base and the way that people have invested in terms of their monies for the long haul. The vast majority of people are compromised to be perfectly honest. They have investment money in all of these things. They're generating income from it, and they're looking forward to these funds for retirement. So many of these people, although they may find themselves somewhat opposed, all of a sudden they go, "Oh, I don't know" and they back off.

*People can't be too opposed?*

(DN) That's right, that's an extremely hard thing to get past. Even within the union movement there are unions that have large pensions funds, and those large pension funds are invested in many of these varied things. And we have had several of them that have withdrawn their funds from Enbridge and from a number of things over the years, because of the awareness that has been brought forward. But it also makes it very hard to organize, it makes it very hard to bring people out. They will sign a document, they will support your initiative, but they won't show their faces, they won't come out. And when you see a crowd of fifteen to thirty people, really they represent each one of them a hundred individuals that won't come out. But that's not how it's viewed within the constraints of the political system or within the media. And it makes it harder to really create any kind of opposition.

*Specifically on Enbridge, the fishermen's union has come out against it, and the Alberta Federation of Labour has come out against it. Are there any other local labour groups that have come out against it?*

(DN) The teacher's union has been quite active in regards to that. They've reviewed their union packages in terms of pensions, that sort of thing.

*Are there any connections between labour and First Nations communities?*

(DN) Very much so. First Nations groups here are involved in the fishery and have always been part of organized labour, either through the United Fishermen and Allied Workers Union or through the Native Brotherhood of B.C. So all of these people have been involved in organized labour, they understand the need to organize, they understand what benefits those organizations provide for them. But that's diminishing because as the fishery diminishes the people that work in it diminishes. New people that come in only work a couple of weeks in the summer; the young kids, they have no concept. We now have almost two generations removed from the fishery in terms of people actively involved. And as such you begin to lose that tie, and that's what it all comes down to, breaking that tie.

I consider myself privileged in many respects. I had the good fortune over the years to have lived a life where I could provide for my family without having to indenture myself in any fashion, either to companies or to any other entities. I'm a free agent and that means I can do whatever I damn well please.

*In this whole situation that you find yourselves in, do you find the academics have any use or they kind of useless?*

(DN) Over my nine years now in this office, you are probably the twenty-fifth or twenty-sixth academic interview that has come through this office. I take advantage of opportunities with each and every one of them. I think academia is a great place. Problem is that it is disappears inside academia, really doesn't resurface anywhere substantial, it remains within academia. If nothing else, I've decided that our lives should be chronicled, so that at least when we're gone somebody will know "We were here". Right now we don't exist anymore anywhere, and that's a scary thing. I spent the last two years mapping traditional fishing knowledge from fishermen here. I have probably several hundred years' worth of fishing knowledge mapped. That's coming from guys who have fished upwards of sixty years. If you take a look at those maps from when those guys started fishing, sixty plus years ago, and take a look at what once constituted the fishery on this coast and what now constitutes the fishery on this coast, it's very scary and many would have you believe that it's strictly conservation. Most of it has been through management, directed from the department for closures and their inability to carry out their mandate, the lack of funding, a range of things have happened to design the fishery that we presently have. Most of them have been economic constraints; it's very little to do with biology. So we have a resource here that's sustainable, that we could continue to generate an immense amount of wealth from for a lot of people but not in large amounts for a single person, and that's the problem. We're now trying to make this resource pay somebody a huge amount of money and that's not the case. When I fished I was very happy with $40,000 a year, which would pay my expenses, that raised my family and we lived relatively well. Still meant that I had to chop my firewood. I had to do a range of other things to add to that, but the fish I brought home offset those costs. And you could live a decent life and not really be a drain on society or the resource in any fashion. That's what fishing is all about, fishing has never been a single economy. It's been an economy that was part of a greater economy. We all had two or three jobs. My early years of fishing I could fish year-round and I could make a substantial amount of money if I so chose to. But it's not much fun being out there in the middle of winter fishing, I can tell you. It's not a pretty place to be. I've stood before Senate committees in Ottawa. I've presented all over this bloody country to various organizations and factions, trying to get people to understand that we are not an industry, We are individual owner-operators and for some reason the east coast has managed to garner that understanding from the rest of the nation. It's considered a fishing end of the country. Therefore, let them keep fishing. So they've left them alone for the most part, and they've allowed them their freedom to this point. But they are coming for them.

Afterword

# The Return of Extractivism
## Henry Veltmeyer & Paul Bowles

Since the early days of capitalist development — the era of mercantilism, colonial rule and the construction of Canada and other nation-states — both capitalism and imperialism have evolved, assuming different forms over time. The latest form of capitalism has been dubbed 'neoliberal globalization' with reference to the 'new world order' established in the early eighties to govern relations of international trade within the world capitalist system and also a program of 'structural reforms' (privatization, liberalization of flows of capital and the movement of tradable products, deregulation of markets and private activity) in macroeconomic policy — rules designed to liberate the 'forces of economic freedom' (the market, the private sector) from the regulatory constraints of the welfare-development state.

The neoliberal policy reform agenda of capitalist development was advanced in three stages. The first cycle of neoliberal reform, implemented under the Washington Consensus on the virtues of free market capitalism, unfolded in the eighties (both at the centre and on the periphery of the system). The result of these 'structural' and institutional reforms in macroeconomic policy was the inability of governments on the periphery of the world capitalist system to protect their domestic producers and industry in the form of industrial policy which had served the now industrialized countries so well in the past.

Bereft of the policy tools (such as public investment, regulations and tariffs) to protect domestic producers and industry, which was the price set for of admission into the new world order, economies on the periphery (in Latin America for example) were subjected to powerful forces that resulted in the destruction of their productive capacity in both agriculture and industry. By the end of the decade, a decade for Latin America 'lost to development' (zero growth in GDP and a decline in per capital incomes), the labour market for wage-paying jobs had effectively been closed down, forcing the masses of dispossessed rural migrants fleeing to the city in the search for a better life to work for themselves 'on their own account' in the streets. Social inequalities in the distribution of income dramatically expanded to the extremes of concentrated wealth at one pole and new forms of (urban) poverty at the other.

The second cycle of neoliberal reforms can be traced back to the early 1990s, with the recognition that policy-makers had gone too far in the direction of the free market, and the perceived need to establish a 'better balance' between the market and the state, i.e., to bring the state back into the development process to secure thereby a more inclusive form of development. This post-Washington Consensus was reached at the beginning of the 1990s, but it was not until the turn into the new millennium that it crystallized in the form of a 'new social policy' oriented towards poverty reduction as well as a new economic model designed to bring about a more inclusive form of development — the 'new developmentalism', as it is termed in Latin America.

However, conditions in the new millennium had radically changed with the third cycle, characterized by a major influx of capital in the form of foreign direct investment, but also the growth of a popular movement led by peasants, landless rural workers and Indigenous communities, opposed to the neoliberal policy agenda.

In some countries, the new economic model constructed in the wake of these social movements was geared to changing conditions both inside the region (the widespread rejection of neoliberalism as an economic doctrine and guide to public policy) and in the world economy, where the ascent of China as an economic power and a source of the growing demand for 'commodities', including precious metals, energy and industrial minerals, has been central to the return to extractivism in many parts of the world. Under these conditions the political class on the left in a number of countries managed to achieve state power, elected by a populace anxious to move beyond neoliberalism and to demand an improvement in their social condition. The result was the construction of a post-neoliberal state in a number of countries in South America — Venezuela (1999), Brazil (2002), Argentina (2003), Chile and Bolivia (2006), Ecuador (2007) and Paraguay (2008).

Under pressure from the outside and within, many of the governments formed within the institutional and policy framework of this state turned towards the 'new developmentalism' and a strategy of national development based on the extraction of natural resources and the export of these resources in primary commodity form: extractivism and reprimarization (the return towards primary commodity exports). The policies of these post-neoliberal regimes were characterized by 'inclusionary state activism' — the channelling of resource rents and fiscal revenues into anti-poverty social programs. The new extractivism.

However, these post-neoliberal regimes were not the only ones to turn towards extractivism as a strategy of national development — 'sustainable resource development' in the discourse of the Canadian government. Extractivism has been followed by both post-neoliberal and neoliberal states, by parties of the right and of the left. For example, both Colombia and Mexico, regimes that were aligned with the U.S. and held steadfastly to the Washington Consensus and the neoliberal model, also turned towards extractivism as a development strategy — a strategy to which Canadian mining companies in particular responded by dramatically expanding investments and operations in Latin America. And in Canada, a similar development was occurring, with the federal government, for example, turning away from policies designed to expand the forces of national production in Canada's industrial heartland and towards a strategy of natural resource development — extracting the country's wealth of natural resources, such as tarsands oil, which were predominantly concentrated in the west rather than the east (Ontario and Quebec) — creating not only a new axis of capitalist development but also the regionalization of national politics. The rush to send natural resources to Asia is as keenly felt in Canada, and in northern B.C. in particular, as it is many Latin American countries.

Extractivism (natural resource extraction and the export of commodities) in its classical and new forms has therefore come to dominate economic and political developments in Canada and other parts of the world over the past decade. The economic impact of extractivism can be traced out in the pattern of global capital flows — the flow of foreign direct investment, portfolio investments and large-scale operations and speculative investments of international financial institutions and commodity traders. For example, Latin America over the past decade has received a disproportionate share of the global flows of foreign direct investments, and a large and increasing share of these investments are 'resource seeking' — in the search of profitable returns on the extraction of resources and commodity exports. Another result of this turn towards extractivism is what the World Bank has called 'large-scale foreign investment in the acquisition of land', more accurately labelled 'land grabbing' (the purchase by both corporations and governments of large tracts of land) in Africa and parts of Latin America and Asia for the purpose of growing food, producing biofuels and extracting natural resources in the form of precious metals and minerals — to meet the food and energy security needs back home.

Canada has actively participated in this development process, particularly as regards the operations of Canadian mining companies, which now dominate extractive operations and global trade in precious metals, accounting today for up to 60 percent of all the investments in this sector worldwide. In Latin America, for example, Canadian mining companies are now the major player in the flow of foreign direct investments and mining operations in the region. To pave the way for the investments and operations of Canadian mining companies and to provide maximum financial and other forms of support for these operations, the Canadian government has become a major player in providing funding and both political and diplomatic support to Canadian mining companies, to help them in their negotiations with local governments and their conflicts with the communities negatively impacted by mining operations. In addition to the use of 'foreign aid' funds, channelled through CIDA, Canada's agency for 'international cooperation', in support of Canadian mining companies in their overseas operations, the Canadian government has played a major role in creating an overarching framework of rules to govern international trade in natural resources and commodities, a regime of 'corporate social responsibility' and a model of 'sustainable resource development'.

Notwithstanding the numerous contradictions and serious negative economic effects (including the impacts on manufacturing and value-added jobs in general) and political effects (including the privileging of large capitalist extractivist firms and foreign investors) of extractivism as a strategy of national development, they pale in comparison with their negative social and environmental impacts. Numerous scientific studies on these impacts have demonstrated a pattern of livelihood destruction and environmental degradation, as well as negative effects on the health of the population directly affected by the operations of extractive capitalism, including open pit mining, gold and silver mining, the construction and operations of oil and gas pipelines, and tanker traffic.

These impacts have been so severe as to lead many analysts to view them as a new form of 'accumulation by dispossession' — accumulating capital (making private profit) by reducing access of communities across the world on the periphery of world capitalism, including northern B.C., to the global commons of land and water (and resources), forcing those directly impacted by extractive operations — and the new global landgrab and resource grab — to abandon their ways of life and their communities.

As for the negative environmental impacts, a report by U.S. and European environmental groups documented the effects of mining-related toxins on populations and communities in different parts of the world, including Argentina, Nigeria and Indonesia. Parts of Argentina, according to this report, are among the top ten most polluted places on the planet as the direct result of mining activities, gold mining for example, that use mercury and cyanide in the processing of the precious metal. In these extraordinarily toxic places, the report adds, 'lifespans are short and disease runs rampant', and once these toxins are released into the environment they can leach into watersheds and end up in fish and other foods people eat anywhere on the planet, converting a local problem into a global issue.[3]

Another dimension of socio-environmental impacts of extractive capitalism and of relevance to this book, are oil pipeline breaks and oil spills. For example, in

---

3    See Stephen Leahy, "Toxic towns and poisoned rivers: a byproduct of industry for the rich," theguardian.co.uk, Friday 8 November, 2013.

tracking Canada's history of pipeline spills Kheraj made reference to a CBC *News* report on Canada's system of gas and oil pipelines, which documented 1,047 sep-arate pipeline spills ('Pipe Line Leaks, Breaks, and Malfunctions') between 2000 and 2011.[4] As for Enbridge, which operates the world's longest crude oil and liquids pipeline system, with data culled from Enbridge's own reports, the Polaris Institute calculated that from 1999 to 2010 up to 804 spills occurred on Enbridge pipelines.[5] And this is in the case of a company that takes pride in being an industry leader in corporate social responsibility and in the use of the most advanced technology regarding the tools, technologies, and strategies necessary to ensure the fitness of its pipelines and the prevention and maintenance as well as the cleanup of oil spills.

It is no wonder that the Voices in this book are unanimous in their view that the proposed oil pipeline and the associated tanker traffic have no place on the land and waters of northern British Columbia. And in their resistance they speak as part of a wider national and global movement.

---

4   Sean Kheraj, "Tracking Canada's History of Oil Pipeline Spills," ActiveHistory.ca, November 7, 2013

5   See Richard Girard, Out on the Tar Sands Mainline: Mapping Enbridge's Web of Pipelines, Polaris Institute, March 2012.

# Acknowledgements

We would like to express our thanks to all those who participated in interviews with us during our journey along the proposed pipeline route. Many of those interviews appear in this book but others do not; we found all of them extremely informative and thank all participants. We also acknowledge funding from the Social Sciences and Humanities Research Council of Canada for a grant supporting a larger project called "Globalizing Northern British Columbia."

The editors also wish to acknowledge with appreciation the interest of Fernwood Publishing, especially Errol Sharpe and Beverley Rach, in the project and their efforts to get it into production so expeditiously.

We should also like to add our appreciation to Fiona MacPhail and Annette Wright, our life partners, for their contributions to our own efforts to put together this publication.